POLICY DIALOGUE No. 14

SADC – THE SOUTHERN ARRESTED DEVELOPMENT COMMUNITY?

Enduring Challenges to Peace and Security in Southern Africa

Author
Michael Aeby

NORDISKA AFRIKAINSITUTET
The Nordic Africa Institute

UPPSALA 2019

INDEXING TERMS:

Southern Africa
Regional development
Regional cooperation
Governance
African organizations
Conflict management
Peace
Peacekeeping
Regional security
Southern African Development
Community

SADC – The Southern Arrested Development Community?
Enduring Challenges to Peace and Security in Southern Africa
Policy Dialogue No. 14

Author: Michael Aeby

ISBN 978-91-7106-853-8 print
ISBN 978-91-7106-854-5 pdf

ISSN 1654-9090 print
ISSN 1654-6790 pdf

Language editor: Clive Liddiard
Layout and production editor: Henrik Alfredsson
Print on demand: Lightning Source UK Ltd.

Front cover: Train in Mozambique, May 2011.
Photo: Nina May, Flickr.

THE NORDIC AFRICA INSTITUTE conducts independent, policy-relevant research, provides analysis and informs decision-making, with the aim of advancing research-based knowledge of contemporary Africa. The institute is jointly financed by the governments of Finland, Iceland and Sweden.

Contents

Map illustration: Henrik Alfredsson, the Nordic Africa Institute

The Southern African Development Community (SADC) has 16 member states.

1. Introduction

The majority of countries in the Southern African Development Community (SADC) have been generally peaceful and stable in recent years; however, the region continues to grapple with a series of violent intrastate conflicts and latent security risks. This policy dialogue report reviews some of the major challenges to peace and security that the region has faced in the past few years, as well as the development of SADC's peace and security architecture and responses to crises in member states.

The relative stability of the Southern African region at present is remarkable, considering its long history of violent, large-scale conflict. Not only was Southern Africa the last part of the continent to be freed from colonialism – through armed liberation struggles, which continue to shape its politics and societies – but the region also suffered from intertwined proxy and civil wars that, in some instances, outlived the Cold War. By pursuing a concerted strategy of deliberately destabilising African states that harboured liberation movements and fuelling intrastate conflicts north of its borders, the South African apartheid regime undermined peace and development in the region, and prompted its neighbours to form a defensive alliance.[1] Both SADC's peace and security architecture, which emerged from this historic alliance of Frontline States, and the Community as such were put to the test in the late 1990s, when several SADC states became embroiled in 'Africa's World War', which raged in the Democratic Republic of the Congo (DRC).[2]

Whilst armed conflict continues in the eastern DRC, the generally peaceful SADC region nowadays boasts a number of stable democracies and prosperous economies. Moreover, in the past 20 years, SADC institutions have taken on an important role in managing matters of regional peace and security, including crises in member states. Major crises and risks in the region presently relate to armed insurgencies, weak institutions, poor governance, democratic deficits and unstable governments, as well as enduring socio-economic grievances that give rise to social conflicts and undermine human security. In addition to the war against multiple rebel groups in the DRC, the region has seen the rekindling of armed insurgencies in Angola and Mozambique.[3]

Constitutional crises resulting from the undermining of democratic institutions by authoritarian regimes and the military have been temporarily contained through the

---

1 Africa, Sandy and Molomo, Mpho, 'Security in southern Africa: The state of the debate', in A. Van Nieuwkerk and K. Hofmann (eds), Southern African Security Review 2013 (Maputo, Friedrich Ebert Stiftung, 2013), p. 17.

2 Khadiagala, Gilbert M., 'The SADCC and its approaches to African regionalism', in C. Saunders, G.A. Dzinesa and D. Nagar (eds), Region-Building in Southern Africa: Progress, problems and prospects (London, Zed Books, 2012), pp. 25–28; Nathan, Laurie, Community of Insecurity: SADC's struggle for peace and security in Southern Africa (Farnham, Ashgate Publishing, 2012), pp. 23, 38, 45.

3 International Crisis Group (ICG), Crisis Watch Database, 30.9.17, www.crisisgroup.org/crisiswatch/database

formation of transitional governments in Zimbabwe, Madagascar and the DRC.[4] But the enduring crisis of governance in Zimbabwe escalated into a coup d'état and the authoritarian government has continued to resort to violence and repression against opponents. Notwithstanding a change of leadership, the legitimacy crisis of the DRC government could not be resolved either as an interregnum culminated in disputed elections.[5] Meanwhile, eSwatini (formerly Swaziland) remains an absolute monarchy with severe governance deficits, and Lesotho continues to suffer from political instability and military interference in civilian politics. Governance deficits, political conflicts and electoral violence are also affecting South Africa's consolidated democracy and otherwise peaceful states like Zambia.[6]

The region's economic hegemon, South Africa, and states that have experienced rapid economic growth, including Angola and Mozambique, face the formidable challenge of promoting social transformation, steering resource rents towards poverty alleviation, and tackling tremendous economic inequities. Given the slow pace of economic transformation in the post-apartheid era, social unrest – which in its most extreme manifestations has resulted in violent clashes with police and recurring xenophobic attacks – has become more pronounced in South Africa in recent years.[7]

In addition to the Organ for Politics, Defence and Security, which was incorporated into the SADC framework in 1996, SADC has established a set of institutions that, together with the relevant structures of the African Union (AU) and other regional economic communities, form part of the African Peace and Security Architecture (APSA).[8] The development of SADC's peace and security institutions is faltering, however, and the structures that have been created thus far need greater political support,

---

4 Aeby, Michael, 'Stability and sovereignty at the expense of democracy? The SADC mediation mandate for Zimbabwe, 2007–2013', African Security, 10, 3–4 (2017), p. 272; Witt, Antonia, 'Mandate impossible: Mediation and the return to constitutional order in Madagascar (2009–13)', African Security, 10, 3–4 (2017), pp. 205–07; Antonia Witt, interview, 12.12.17.

5 Sabelo Ndlovu-Gatsheni, interview via Skype, 2.12.17; Wolters, Stephanie, 'Without elections, the DRC's economy will continue to slide', Institute for Security Studies, Pretoria (2017).

6 International Crisis Group (ICG), Crisis Watch Database, 30.9.17; Matlosa, Khabele, 'The state of democratisation in Southern Africa: Blocked transitions, reversals, stagnation, progress and prospects', Politikon, 44, 1 (2017), pp. 5–26; Southall, Roger, 'The coming crisis of Zuma's ANC: The party state confronts fiscal crisis', Review of African Political Economy, 43, 147 (2016), pp. 73–88; Vandome, Christopher, Vines, Alex and Weimer, Markus, Swaziland: Southern Africa's forgotten crisis (London, Chatham House, 2013).

7 Mkhize, Mbekezeli C., 'Is South Africa's 20 years of democracy in crisis? Examining the impact of unrest incidents in local protests in the post-apartheid South Africa', African Security Review, 24, 2 (2015), pp. 190–206; Perez Nino, Helena and Le Billon, Philippe, 'Foreign aid, resource rents, and state fragility in Mozambique and Angola', Annals of the American Academy of Political and Social Science, 656, 1 (2014), pp. 79–96; Vines, Alex, Thompson, Henry, Jensen, Soren Kirk and Azevedo-Harman, Elisabete, Mozambique to 2018: Managers, mediators and magnates (London, Chatham House, 2015), pp. 14–15.

8 Van Nieuwkerk, Anthoni, 'Exploring SADC's evolving peace and security policy framework', in A. Van Nieuwkerk and K. Hofmann (eds), Southern African Security Review 2013 (Maputo, Friedrich Ebert Stiftung, 2013), pp. 37–53.

organisational capacity and more resources.[9] While SADC has responded to a series of intrastate crises since its formation in 1992, both the outcome of these interventions and its record on promoting peace and the democratic principles enshrined in its founding documents have been mixed.[10] In the recent past, SADC has responded decisively to military interference and government instability in the dwarf state of Lesotho, sanctioning the deployment of troops.[11] But SADC's muted response to the DRC's constitutional crisis, which arose from a failure to hold timely elections before President Laurent Kabila's term of office expired, the interference by the Zimbabwean army in civilian politics, which compelled President Robert Mugabe to resign, and several disputed elections signals both a continued inability and an unwillingness on the part of SADC to consistently enforce its liberal democratic founding principles.[12]

The primary objective of this report, commissioned by the Nordic Africa Institute (NAI), is to provide an overview of political, economic and social developments in SADC member states, in order to assess the implications that these issues may have for peace and security in the SADC region. The second key objective is to review SADC's peace and security architecture and the organisation's responses to the crises in member states, and to gauge its ability to effectively manage regional peace and security challenges. The report, therefore, seeks to address the following guiding questions: What implications do the selected political, economic and social developments in SADC states have for peace and security at both the national and the regional level? To what extent has SADC's peace and security architecture been operationalised, and how effective are its institutions in their present shape? How has SADC responded to the intrastate crises discussed, and how effective have these responses been in terms of containing the escalation of violent conflict and promoting peace and security in the region?

To research these questions, the main part of this study is structured into three sections concerned with (1) longer-term regional trends and enduring peace and security challenges; (2) the development of SADC's peace and security institutions and policies; and (3) a selection of recent intrastate crises, security risks and SADC responses to conflicts in member states. The enduring challenges discussed in this report relate to armed conflicts; matters of governance, including elections and the transition of state power; and social and economic issues that have the potential to fuel violent conflict

9 Laurie Nathan, interview by email, 2.12.17.

10 Lins De Albuquerque, Adriana and Hull Wiklund, Cecilia, Challenges to Peace and Security in Southern Africa: The role of SADC (Stockholm, Swedish Defence Research Agency, 2015). https://www.foi.se/download/18.7fd35d7f166c56ebe0bb390/1542369060270/Challenges-to-Peace-and-Security-in-S-Africa_The-Role-of-SADC_FOI-Memo-5594.pdf), pp. 1–4; Nathan, Community of Insecurity, pp. 1–12.

11 International Crisis Group (ICG), Crisis Watch Database, 30.9.17; SADC, Double Troika Summit Communiqué, Pretoria, 15.9.17.

12 SADC, Executive Secretary Stergomena Lawrence Tax, SADC Congratulates His Excellency Emmerson Dambudzo Mnangagwa, President of the Republic of Zimbabwe, Gaborone, 24.11.17; SADC, Organ Troika Communiqué, Luanda, 21.11.17; SADC, Summit Communiqué, Pretoria, 20.8.17.

and undermine stability. The overview of SADC's institutional framework and policies for regional peace and security discusses the legacies of its institutional predecessors, the development and workings of key institutions, including the Organ for Politics, Defence and Security, the implementation of the Strategic Indicative Plan for the Organ, the operationalisation of the SADC component of the APSA, as well as regional dynamics and norms informing SADC's conflict management in practice.

Finally, the study discusses recent armed, political and social conflicts, as well as human security risks in Mozambique, Angola and Zimbabwe. The conflicts and risks that are discussed have been selected because of their severity and potential impact on peace and security in the region as a whole. While it discusses the respective conflicts in their historical context, the analysis focuses on the period since 2013, when the region saw several key developments that marked a significant change in the overall political situation. These included the end of the SADC-brokered transitional governance processes in Madagascar and Zimbabwe; the escalation of the armed insurgency in Mozambique; and the quelling of the M23 rebellion in eastern DRC. The discussion of the above intrastate crises includes a review of SADC's responses to these challenges. The findings pertaining to the intrastate conflicts and security risks discussed, to SADC's crisis management and to the relevant SADC structures will be synthesised in the conclusion.

As the desk study covers multiple security challenges in a range of countries, and as it seeks to provide a regional overview, the analysis relies on available literature, interviews with experts and news coverage of the peace and security challenges discussed. The study, moreover, analyses SADC policy documents and communiqués released during the period of analysis, to trace SADC's crisis responses.

Most of the acute intrastate crises of the last ten years in SADC countries have been prompted by matters of governance.

Chapter 2, page 15

Cabo Delgado Province, Mozambique, 1972 (exact date unknown).
Makonde wood-carvers at work in a Frelimo production camp.
Photo: N Basom, UN Photo.

2. Regional trends and enduring challenges

Armed conflict: from regional wars to local insurgencies

The three types of contemporary peace and security challenges in the SADC region that are discussed in this report – armed insurgencies, matters of governance and democracy, and socio-economic development – have their roots in Southern Africa's violent colonial and post-colonial past. Southern Africa has gradually evolved from a region racked by large-scale wars to one of the most peaceful parts of Africa. Between the 1970s and the turn of the millennium, the region experienced a range of anti-colonial and civil wars, some of which took on characteristics of proxy wars during the Cold War and apartheid era. Zimbabwe attained its independence in 1980, after a war of liberation against the Rhodesian white minority regime, and experienced state-sponsored mass atrocities during an asymmetric civil war in the 1980s.[13] In Mozambique and Angola – both of which endured anti-colonial wars up until independence in 1975 – civil war continued until 1992 and 2002, respectively, between the (formerly) Soviet-aligned governments and rebels who were supported by apartheid South Africa. The demise of the apartheid regime in the global geopolitical setting of the post-Cold War era, and the end of its total strategy of destabilising African states and waging war to secure its northern frontier, brought about peace processes in Mozambique and Angola – although in the latter country, this process collapsed in the wake of the 1992 elections.[14] Two years earlier, international pressure had resulted in the end of the long-standing South African occupation of Namibia, from where South Africa had waged its border war, and in Namibia's independence.[15] In South Africa itself, violent clashes between supporters of the competing African nationalist parties – clashes that were clandestinely sponsored by the decaying regime and drove the divided nation further apart – continued at an enormous cost in human life throughout the country's negotiated transition (1990–1994).[16]

---

13 Mtisi, Joseph, Nyakudya, Munyaradzi and Barnes, Teresa, 'War in Rhodesia, 1965–1980', in B. Raftopoulos and A. Mlambo (eds), *Becoming Zimbabwe: A history from the pre-colonial period to 2008* (Harare and Johannesburg, Weaver/Jacana, 2009), pp. 141–66; Phimister, Ian, 'The makings and meanings of the massacres in Matabeleland', *Development Dialogue*, 50 (2008), pp. 179–234.

14 Birmingham, David, 'Angola', in P. Chabal (ed.), *A History of Postcolonial Lusophone Africa* (London, Indiana University Press, 2002), pp. 137–84.

15 Saunders, Chris, 'Mediation mandates for Namibia's independence (1977–78, 1988)', *African Security*, 10, 3–4 (2017), pp. 245–49; Vines, Alex, 'Renamo's rise and decline: The politics of reintegration in Mozambique', *International Peacekeeping*, 20, 3 (2013), p. 376.

16 Sparks, Allister, *Tomorrow is Another Country: The inside story of South Africa's negotiated settlement* (Cape Town and Johannesburg, 1995), pp. 124, 155–60; *Truth and Reconciliation Commission Report of South Africa* (Cape Town, 1998), Vol. 2, p. 577; Simpson, James G.R., 'Boipatong: The politics of a massacre and the South African transition', *Journal of Southern African Studies*, 38, 3 (2012), pp. 623–28.

While South Africa embarked on an arduous path towards reconciliation, after holding its first democratic election in 1994, the regional reverberations of the Rwandan genocide and the imminent collapse of the long-standing Zairian regime set the stage for the devastating Congo wars that heralded an unprecedented humanitarian disaster.[17] SADC became embroiled in the Second Congo War in 1998. Although the SADC Summit was deeply divided over its response, and although a group of heads of state led by South African President Nelson Mandela favoured a diplomatic solution, SADC retroactively sanctioned military intervention by Angola, Namibia and Zimbabwe. Those three states – whose military involvement had been motivated not least by the prospect of economic spoils – came to the rescue of the DRC government of President Gabriel Kabila after he fell out with his Rwandan backers, who had previously elevated him to power. South Africa and its second democratically elected president, Thabo Mbeki, by contrast, would assume a critical role in facilitating an inter-Congolese dialogue, which would lead to the signing of a peace agreement in 2002, the installation of an interim power-sharing government, and a general election in 2006.[18]

The armed conflicts and contemporary peace and security challenges that the SADC region continues to grapple with stem from the above-mentioned history of large-scale conflicts of the colonial and post-colonial era. The fighting in the eastern DRC did not stop with the 2002 Sun City peace agreement. The repeated armed insurgencies that have erupted since the Congo wars have continued to follow a similar logic, in that they are driven by competition over spoils from the exploitation of mineral deposits; local struggles over scarce resources that are at times intertwined with interethnic tensions, some of which relate to the legacies of the Rwandan genocide; the interference of the Rwandan government; banditry; and the weakness of the Congolese state and army.[19] In Mozambique, the armed conflict between the historical belligerents of the civil war – the government of the *Frente de Libertação de Moçambique* (FRELIMO) and the rebels of the *Resistência Nacional Moçambicana* (RENAMO) – erupted anew in 2012. Meanwhile, the separatist insurgency in Angola's Cabinda province, which flared up again in 2016, dates back to the colonial period.[20]

---

17 Turner, Thomas, The Congo Wars: Conflict, myth, and reality (London, Zed Books, 2007), pp. 75–77; Weiss, Herbert and Carayannis, Tatiana, 'Reconstructing the Congo', Journal of International Affairs, 58, 1 (2004), pp. 115–23.

18 Curtis, Devon, 'South Africa: "Exporting peace" to the Great Lakes Region?', in A. Adebajo, A. Adedeji and C. Landsberg (eds), South Africa in Africa: The post-apartheid era (Pietermaritzburg, University of KZN Press, 2007), p. 262; Kabemba, Claude, 'South Africa and the DRC: Is a stable and developmental state possible in the Congo?', in S. Roger (ed.), South Africa's Role in Conflict Resolution and Peacemaking in Africa (Cape Town, HSRC Press, 2006), pp. 158–64; Nathan, Community of Insecurity, pp. 86–91.

19 Vlassenroot, Koen and Mathys, Gillian, '"It's not all about the land": Land disputes and conflict in the eastern Congo', Rift Valley Institute, PSRP Briefing Paper 14 (2016), p. 1; Verweijen Judith, Stable Instability: Political settlements and armed groups in the Congo (London, Rift Valley Institute, 2016), pp. 7–10; Turner, Thomas, 'Will Rwanda end its meddling in Congo?', Current History, 112, 754 (2013), p. 188; Hoffmann, Kasper, Vlassenroot, Koen and Marchais, Gauthier, 'Taxation, stateness and armed groups: Public authority and resource extraction in eastern Congo', Development and Change, 47, 6 (2016), p. 1434.

20 Didier Péclard, interview via email, 8.12.17; Vines, 'Renamo's rise and decline', p. 376.

Besides these comparatively minor insurgencies in the Lusophone states, the ongoing warfare in the DRC, and the societal scars from the era of anti-colonial and civil conflicts, the once war-riven Southern African region has overcome its long history of armed conflict. Moreover, in contrast to the closely intertwined large-scale wars of the Cold War and the armed struggle against white minority regimes, Southern Africa's contemporary conflicts are, with the exception of the eastern DRC and a non-violent border dispute between Malawi and Tanzania, overwhelmingly of a national rather than an international nature.[21]

The quality of governance and democracy

Most of the acute intrastate crises of the last ten years in SADC countries have been prompted by matters of governance, including electoral stalemates, authoritarian rule, government unaccountability, and the abuse of state resources for the preservation of power. These are equally rooted in the violent struggles of the past. The majority of countries in Southern Africa are governed by former underground guerrilla movements, which took charge of repressive colonial states that were designed to suit the interests of European settler populations. The liberation generation of Southern African political elites – in whose experience political power was won through the barrel of a gun – was politically socialised in the context of armed struggle and colonial oppression; and it continues to govern a number of states in the region. The liberation movements needed to make the transition from guerrilla armies and underground organisations to political parties capable of engaging in statecraft and electoral politics. The war-time political socialisation of elites and liberation movement legacies of the parties in power account to a considerable extent for the continued authoritarian traits, lack of democratic values, commando style of governance and militaristic culture of several Southern African governments, as well as for the involvement of the security sector in civilian affairs and party politics. While some liberation-party governments have made considerable strides in rolling out social services to the majority of the population and in transforming state institutions, at independence the liberation-party elites took control of the coercive apparatus of the authoritarian settler states and not infrequently used these instruments to crush opponents, entrench themselves in power and accumulate wealth. Furthermore, both the political and military elites that had dedicated themselves to liberating their countries from racist settler regimes, and the political organisations that regarded themselves as 'vanguard' parties, developed a sense of entitlement to power, privilege and state resources. The most obstinate military and liberation-party elites equate the loss of state power with a reversal of the achievements of the liberation struggle. These liberation hardliners are, therefore, determined to retain state power by all means possible; and conceding defeat in an election is un-

21 Africa and Molomo, 'Security in southern Africa', p. 22; Van Nieuwkerk, Anthoni, 'The strategic culture of foreign and security policymaking: Examining the Southern African Development Community', African Security, 7, 1 (2014), p. 58.

acceptable to them, no matter how little popular support their party may still enjoy. The notion that those parties that waged the liberation struggle are entitled to state power – something that is characteristic of this type of liberation ideology – has, in some instances, rendered government elites unaccountable to the population they are meant to serve.[22] The sense of entitlement may also allow liberation-party elites, who 'did not join the struggle to be poor',[23] to justify the use of political power in order to acquire personal wealth.

The above tendencies that stem from liberation-party legacies and their detrimental impact on the quality of governance, democratic processes, peace and stability are, arguably, most pronounced in the case of the long-standing regime of the Zimbabwe African National Union-Patriotic Front (ZANU-PF). Since the outbreak of Zimbabwe's political and economic crisis at the turn of the millennium, the ZANU-PF government has systematically deployed an anti-imperialist African nationalist discourse that legitimises its continued grip on power by recalling its efforts in the liberation struggle, and that denigrates its domestic opponents as Western agents seeking to restore white minority rule. The partisan leadership of the Zimbabwe Defence Forces (ZDF) – which has been involved in the illicit siphoning off of national resources and mass violence against civilians – has repeatedly declared that it would never accept a government lacking liberation-struggle credentials, and derailed the 2008 electoral process in order to keep ZANU-PF in power.[24] In 2017, the Zimbabwean generals justified their blatant intervention in civilian politics – designed to ensure that Robert Mugabe was succeeded as president by the struggle veteran Emmerson Mnangagwa, rather than by a candidate supported by the younger generation of ZANU-PF elites – as an operation to restore the legacy of the liberation struggle.[25]

The manifestations of the phenomena relating to liberation-party governments described here vary markedly across the region and are generally less problematic than in the case of Zimbabwe. But the authoritarian traits, the sense of entitlement and the use of a liberation discourse to legitimise the perpetuation of political power can be observed in a number of Southern African states, as illustrated by the work of a range

22 Elísio Macamo, interview, Basel, 22.11.17; Sabelo Ndlovu-Gatsheni, interview via Skype, 2.12.17; Didier Péclard, interview via email, 8.12.17; Ndlovu-Gatsheni, Sabelo, 'ZANU-PF in power in Zimbabwe, 1980–2013: Towards explaining why former liberation movements fail as governments', in R. Bereketeab (ed.), National Liberation Movements as Government in Africa (Abingdon, Routledge, 2017), pp. 122–40.

23 The phrase was originally used by Smuts Ngonyama when accused of unfair business practices in 2007 and has since been emblematically used to describe a culture of entitlement in the African National Congress; Holland, Heidi, 'ANC grows older but not wiser', The Star, 3.1.12.

24 Aeby, Michael, 'Zimbabwe's gruelling transition: Interim power-sharing and conflict management in Southern Africa', University of Basel (2015), pp. 46–48, 52–56, 108, 350; Masunungure, Eldred V., 'A militarized election: The 27 June presidential run-off', in E.V. Masunungure (ed.), Defying the Winds of Change: Zimbabwe's 2008 elections (Harare, Weaver Press, 2009), pp. 79–97.

25 Herald, 'The operation to restore legacy', 5.12.17; Raftopoulos, Brian, Caught between the Croc and Gucci City (Cape Town, S.P. Trust, 2017).

of scholars.[26] The *Movimento Popular de Libertação de Angola* (MPLA) portrays itself as the sole legitimate power-holder and embodiment of the nation.[27] The prevalent political culture in Angola, which was shaped by the use of violence and coercion during the anti-colonial struggle, leaves little space for the kind of political competition that is required in a democratic society, impedes the governance of public goods, and has resulted in the establishment of a 'command state' that continues to rely on coercion as a means of governance.[28]

Mozambique's FRELIMO government has generally adhered to democratic principles and has tolerated political competition since the introduction of multi-party democracy, but it has not abandoned its exclusionary logic towards opposition parties and critics.[29] FRELIMO's teleological liberation narrative – which saw the party as the sole legitimate representative of the people and as a communist vanguard party – has left its imprint on Mozambique's post-conflict nation-building project. The messianic liberation-party narrative has led FRELIMO cadres to believe that the nation would fall into the hands of an illegitimate leadership, were the party ever to lose power; this makes it hard for party stalwarts to accept democratic institutions and freedom of expression.[30]

Under the government of the South West African People's Organisation (SWAPO), Namibia has become one of the region's most democratic states and has embraced liberal democratic norms, including competitive elections, freedom of expression, human rights and the rule of law. Different standards of accountability, however, may apply to SWAPO comrades. Shadow networks of the overwhelmingly dominant party work through the state apparatus to promote personal gain, curtail the opposition and tilt the electoral playing field, as SWAPO cadres fail to distinguish between the party, the executive and the state. To legitimise its hegemonic rule, SWAPO, like its Zimbabwean counterpart, has, first of all, articulated an authoritative patriotic history – a selective heroic narrative of the liberation struggle that glorifies SWAPO's deeds, while air-

---

26 Bereketeab, Redie, 'Introduction: Understanding national liberation movements', in R. Bereketeab (ed.), National Liberation Movements as Government in Africa (Abingdon, Routledge, 2017), pp. 1–5; Macamo, Elísio, 'Violence and political culture in Mozambique', Social Dynamics, 42, 1 (2016), pp. 85–105; Melber, Henning, 'Southern African liberation movements as governments and the limits to liberation', Review of African Political Economy, 36, 121 (2009), pp. 451–59; Salih, M.A. Mohamed, 'African Liberation Movement Governments and Democracy', Democratization, 14, 4 (2007), pp. 669–85; Southall, Roger, 'Introduction: Analysing national liberation movements as governments', in R. Southall (ed.), Liberation Movements in Power (Woodbridge, Boydell and Brewer, 2013), pp. 1–16.

27 Didier Péclard, interview via email, 8.12.17.

28 Ingles, Paulo, 'The MPLA government and its post-liberation record in Angola', in R. Bereketeab (ed.), National Liberation Movements as Government in Africa (Abingdon, Routledge, 2017), pp. 45, 55.

29 Nuvunga, Adriano N., 'From former liberation movement to four decades in government: The maintenance of the Frelimo state', in R. Bereketeab (ed.), National Liberation Movements as Government in Africa (Abingdon, Routledge, 2017), p. 67.

30 Macamo, 'Violence and political culture in Mozambique', pp. 85, 100; Elísio Macamo, interview, Basel, 22.11.17.

brushing out its malpractices. Secondly, the party has pursued a nation-building project that equates the national identity to that of SWAPO, and thus situates SWAPO's opponents outside the national community.[31]

The African National Congress (ANC) – which led the struggle against the South African apartheid regime and established liberal electoral democracy via political negotiation rather than military force – has always primarily been a political organisation rather than a liberation army, although its armed wing fought in the border war. Since the days of the anti-apartheid struggle, the political project of the ANC has included what are, in some respects, contradictory discursive traditions of liberal democracy, socialism and African nationalism. The broad-church party continues to be made up of competing forces that promote these different components of the party's identity and objectives. Since the advent of democracy, the ANC has relied heavily on its liberation-struggle credentials to garner electoral support and legitimise its control over state institutions, even as the quality of governance, democracy and accountability to the citizenry have declined, especially during Jacob Zuma's presidency.[32] Having won a comfortable majority in national elections since 1994, thanks to its liberation legacy, elements of the party leadership have adopted the mentality that the 'ANC will rule until Jesus comes',[33] regardless of its performance in government.[34] As the ANC's popularity has waned due to popular frustration with corruption, cronyism and poor service delivery, so ANC cadres have resorted to the anti-imperialist discursive repertoire of the liberation struggle, and party organs have insinuated that the opposition Democratic Alliance (DA) is trying to bring back apartheid.[35] The authoritarian traits of the ANC have often been grossly exaggerated by its critics; nevertheless, long-standing concerns that it may curb the political space, resort to undemocratic means and abandon the principle of non-racialism if it risks losing power have gained relevance, given that the ANC's electoral support has shrunk considerably and the party has lost control of several urban constituencies.[36]

---

31 Melber, Henning, 'Struggle mentality versus democracy: The case of SWAPO of Namibia', in R. Bereketeab (ed.), National Liberation Movements as Government in Africa (Abingdon, Routledge, 2017), pp. 143–56; Ranger, Terence, 'Nationalist historiography, patriotic history and the history of the nation: The struggle over the past in Zimbabwe', Journal of Southern African Studies, 30, 2 (2004), pp. 215–34.

32 De Jager, Nicola and Steenekamp, Cindy Lee, 'The changing political culture of the African National Congress', Democratization, 23, 5 (2016), p. 921; Southall, Roger, 'From liberation movement to party machine? The ANC in South Africa', Journal of Contemporary African Studies, 32, 3 (2014), p. 331; The Economist, 'Why the ANC will win South Africa's election, despite governing poorly', 7.5.14.

33 Business Day, 'ANC will rule SA until Jesus comes back, says Zuma', 15.3.04.

34 Southall, 'From liberation movement to party machine?', p. 331.

35 Bond, Patrick, 'The African National Congress: From liberation movement to neoliberal state manager', in R. Bereketeab (ed.), National Liberation Movements as Government in Africa (Abingdon, Routledge, 2017), pp. 107–21; De Jager and Steenekamp, 'The changing political culture of the African National Congress', p. 921; News24, 'DA a Trojan Horse of apartheid, says ANC', 26.7.16; ANCWL, ANC Statement on the DA Motion to Dissolve Parliament, 10.8.17.

36 Chipkin, Ivor, 'The decline of African nationalism and the state of South Africa', Journal of Southern African Studies, 42, 2 (2016), pp. 221; Southall, 'From liberation movement to party machine?, p. 331.

Countries governed by former liberation movements are not the only ones in the SADC region to encounter governance challenges and democratic deficits that risk potential conflicts. If measured by the standards of liberal democracy, which prioritises political freedoms and electoral competition over social justice, several Southern African liberation-party governments are among the most democratic regimes on the African continent.[37] Khabele Matlosa, who for well over a decade has periodically reviewed the state of democracy in the SADC region, distinguishes between several regime types and democratisation trajectories taken by the countries of the region.[38] In his latest assessment, which considers both the presence of tangible democratic institutions and a democratic political culture as indicators of democratisation, he reaches the following findings: While the vast majority of SADC states have embarked on some form of transition from authoritarian rule to a more democratic regime type, they have taken vastly different trajectories, which are neither linear nor irreversible. While several SADC states have consolidated liberal democracy and a few have made progress over the past 10 years, several others have stagnated or relapsed – and then there is eSwatini, which remains an absolute monarchy and has not even begun a democratic transition. Broad generalisations about the state of democracy in Southern Africa would, therefore, be misleading.[39]

These trajectories mean that eSwatini remains the only *closed authoritarian regime* on Matlosa's spectrum of regime types (i.e. an untransformed autocracy). Angola, the DRC and Zimbabwe, meanwhile, fall into the category of *electoral authoritarian regimes*, which are essentially despotic, but maintain a façade of democracy by holding multi-party elections that are conflict ridden, marked by political violence, and lack credibility and uncertainty in terms of their outcome. Lesotho (notwithstanding its recent woes), Malawi, Mozambique and Tanzania are classified as *electoral democracies*, where democratic processes are being institutionalised and are progressively stabilising, but where democracy has not yet been consolidated. In these states, democracy is largely confined to the process of periodically holding elections, and public political participation remains limited. But these countries have developed stable political multi-party systems and have the potential to become liberal democracies in the foreseeable future, in spite of bouts of occasional political turbulence, especially around election time. Botswana, Mauritius, Namibia, South Africa and Seychelles, finally, qualify as *liberal democracies*. These states are characterised by regular and credible multi-party elections with procedural certainty and relatively uncertain outcomes; the institutional protec-

37 The Economist, Democracy Index 2016, https://infographics.economist.com/2017/DemocracyIndex/, 1.12.17; Puddington, Arch and Roylance, Tyler, Populists and Autocrats: The dual threat to global democracy (Washington, DC, Freedom House, 2017), p. 12.

38 Matlosa, Khabele and Lotshwao, Kebapetse, Political Integration and Democratisation in Southern Africa: Progress, problems and prospects (Johannesburg, EISA, 2010); Matlosa, Khabele, Consolidating Democratic Governance in the SADC Region: Transitions and prospects for consolidation (Johannesburg, EISA, 2008); Matlosa, Khabele, 'Elections and conflict management', in C. Saunders, G.A. Dzinesa and D. Nagar (eds), Region-Building in Southern Africa: Progress, problems and prospects (London, Zed Books, 2012), pp. 78–91.

39 Matlosa, 'The state of democratisation in Southern Africa', pp. 5–26.

tion of the rule of law and human rights; and a culture of constitutionalism. In this group, Botswana, Seychelles and Mauritius are enduring and stable liberal democracies, while Namibia and South Africa have undergone comparatively recent transitions and have yet to consolidate democracy fully. Although fulfilling the formal criteria of liberal democracy, these states still lag far behind with regard to socio-economic transformation and social justice that would give substance to the citizenry's democratic rights and possibly enable positive peace.

Democracy is neither a guarantee of, nor a necessary precondition for, peace and stability. However, the democratic deficits, lack of government accountability and poor governance that continue to bedevil various SADC states constitute a major impediment to regional peace and security in Southern Africa. The detrimental impact of these deficits in the domain of governance and democracy is evidenced by the multitude of intrastate crises over elections, the change of government, the mismanagement of public affairs and the disregard for the aspirations of the citizenry that the SADC region has been grappling with over the past two decades.[40]

Socio-economic development

The third type of peace and security challenges highlighted in this report emanates from issues of socio-economic development that affect human security and carry the risk of violent conflict. In the broader sense, these developmental challenges, which cannot be discussed in detail, may relate to economic development, poverty and social security, food security and humanitarian stability, as well as environmental issues.

The heterogeneous SADC region consists of 'least-developed countries' and agrarian states, as well as emerging nations with diversified economies; they differ vastly in terms of their geography, territorial size, population and economic productivity.[41] By 2016, the population of the SADC region was growing by 2.6% per annum and totalled 327.2 million people; 26.6% of these lived in the DRC, 17.1% in South Africa and 13.3% in Tanzania, the region's three most populous nations. The combined gross domestic product (GDP) of all SADC states was US $559.888 billion:[42] South Africa's GDP ($297.833 billion) dwarfed all but Angola's oil-driven national economy, which itself – with a GDP of $107.462 billion – was more than double the size of SADC's third-biggest economy, Tanzania. However, Tanzania's economy was growing the fastest (7%), while South Africa's was stagnating (0.3%) and eSwatini's was contracting (-0.6%), reducing the average GDP growth rate of the SADC region

40 International Crisis Group (ICG), Crisis Watch Database, 30.9.17.

41 Van Nieuwkerk, Anthoni and Notshulwana, Mxolisi, 'A critical examination of the key factors and trends shaping Southern African peace and security', in A. van Nieuwkerk and C. Moat (eds), Southern African Security Review 2015 (Maputo, Friedrich Ebert Stiftung, 2015), p. 33.

42 Henceforth, unless otherwise stated, all dollar amounts are in US dollars.

to a mere 1.4%.[43] In 2014, mining (15.2%) was the foremost contributor to the region's overall GDP, followed by financial services and business (14.8%), government services (14.6%), wholesale, retail and hospitality (13.1%), manufacturing (10.6%), transport and communication (8.6%), agriculture (7.6%) and construction (6.7%). The seemingly well-developed economic diversification is, however, largely a result of the overwhelming contribution of South Africa's emerging economy to SADC's overall GDP. In reality, the national production of most SADC states depends heavily on extractive industries and agriculture, rather than services, as is common for developing countries.[44] In the DRC, Tanzania and Malawi, agriculture is a key contributor to the GDP, whereas Angola, Botswana and eSwatini rely heavily on extractive industries. Tertiary sector service industries are only dominant in Mauritius and South Africa; they are narrowly ahead in Zimbabwe, whose once diversified economy has shrunk dramatically since the outbreak of the crisis at the turn of the millennium.[45]

In 2016, merchandise trade among SADC states had been rising steadily for nine consecutive years, as regional economic integration constitutes a strategic key objective of SADC. Yet, intra-SADC exports as a percentage of total exports of goods amounted to 24.9% in 2016, and imports to 21.2%. The average external debt of SADC states (which had been increasing steadily over the previous decade) amounted to 41% of GDP, with Mozambique (79.2%), Zimbabwe (64.4%), Namibia (53.8%) and South Africa (48.4%) the most heavily indebted countries. The SADC region had a combined trade deficit of $9 billion, as imports ($123 billion) exceeded exports ($114 billion) for the third consecutive year. South Africa, followed by Angola and the DRC, remained the largest exporter and importer of goods for the SADC region, which identifies trade liberalisation as a key goal in advancing regional economic integration.[46] Although the ease of doing business is better in SADC than elsewhere in Africa, the region's competitiveness, especially with regard to manufacturing, remains low in global terms, as the productivity of Southern African countries is hampered by low levels of education and skills, poor health, comparatively high production costs and political uncertainty.[47]

The difficult macroeconomic environment and sluggish growth rates make it all the harder to create livelihoods for a fast-growing population, to provide the economic opportunities and social services necessary to enable people to exit poverty, and to tackle the formidable challenge of alleviating the social inequities created by segregationist settler regimes and perpetuated in the post-colonial period. Official unemployment rates for the SADC region as a whole (and also for some of the worst affected states,

43 SADC, SADC Selected Economic and Social Indicators 2016, Gaborone 2017, http://www.sadc.int/information-services/sadc-statistics

44 SADC, SADC Statistical Yearbook 2014, http://www.sadc.int/information-services/sadc-statistics

45 SADC, SADC Selected Economic and Social Indicators 2016, Gaborone 2017, http://www.sadc.int/information-services/sadc-statistics; Van Nieuwkerk and Notshulwana, 'A critical examination', p. 35.

46 SADC, SADC Selected Economic and Social Indicators 2016, Gaborone 2017, http://www.sadc.int/information-services/sadc-statistics

47 Van Nieuwkerk and Notshulwana, 'A critical examination', p. 34.

such as Zimbabwe) are unavailable. However, over the past decade, the official unemployment rate of most SADC countries has been rising steadily, except for in Zambia, Mauritius and Seychelles – the Indian Ocean islands were the only states to register single-digit unemployment. In 2015, the official unemployment rate was estimated to be 10.3% in Tanzania, 20% in Botswana, 24.2% in Angola, 25.3% in South Africa and 28% in eSwatini. The livelihood of a large share of the population of SADC countries, however, depends on subsistence farming and informal sector trade, rather than formal employment.[48] By 2015, a vast section of the population lived below the national poverty line in virtually all SADC countries, including eSwatini (63%), Zambia (54%), Angola (36%) and Tanzania (28%). As elsewhere on the continent, poverty levels were generally higher in rural areas, as exemplified by South Africa and Zimbabwe. In 2011, some 55.2% of South African rural dwellers in lived in poverty, while the national poverty rate was 32%. In Zimbabwe, 84.3% of those living in rural areas and 72.3% nationwide were classified as poor. Secondary school enrolment ratios ranged in 2015 from 99% in Seychelles and 90.2% in South Africa to a mere 21.9% in Mozambique and 15% in Malawi.[49] The quality of primary education in South Africa, however, remains poor, owing to the legacy of the apartheid education system, which was designed to cement social inequality along racial lines, and an inability to decisively improve the quality of schooling in the post-apartheid era.[50] In the absence of improved education and economic opportunities for graduates, the countries of the SADC region, where 43.2% of the total population is under the age of 25, are vulnerable to more social unrest in the foreseeable future.[51]

Regardless of the high levels of unemployment and poverty, the SADC region has registered a steady increase in life expectancy from 51.8 years in 2007 to 60.1 years in 2016, thanks to improved nutrition, sanitation and medical interventions.[52] By 2016, an average of 71% of the population of SADC states had access to safe drinking water and 60–98% had access to health care. Yet, poor communities remain highly vulnerable due to high food prices and undernutrition rates. The prevalence of HIV/AIDS, which affects all social classes, is still 11.4% on average, with eSwatini (33.6%) and Lesotho (23.1%) the countries most severely affected by the pandemic.

Food security and agricultural production have been adversely affected by several consecutive years of drought, with the southern part of the region experiencing the most severe drought in 35 years in 2016, while the northern parts were experiencing floods. The above-normal temperatures and lack of rainfall resulted in a large decrease in the areas planted, widespread crop failures, the rationing of water and deteriorating

48 SADC, SADC Statistical Yearbook 2015, http://www.sadc.int/information-services/sadc-statistics

49 SADC, SADC Statistical Yearbook 2015, http://www.sadc.int/information-services/sadc-statistics

50 The Economist, 'South Africa has one of the world's worst education systems', 7.1.17; Tibane, Elias and Lentsoane, Nomfundo (eds), South Africa Yearbook 2015/16 (Pretoria, Government Communications, Republic of South Africa, 2016), pp. 133–39.

51 SADC, SADC Regional Vulnerability Assessment and Analysis Synthesis Report 2016 (Gaborone, 2016), p. 9.

52 SADC, SADC Statistical Yearbook 2015, http://www.sadc.int/information-services/sadc-statistics

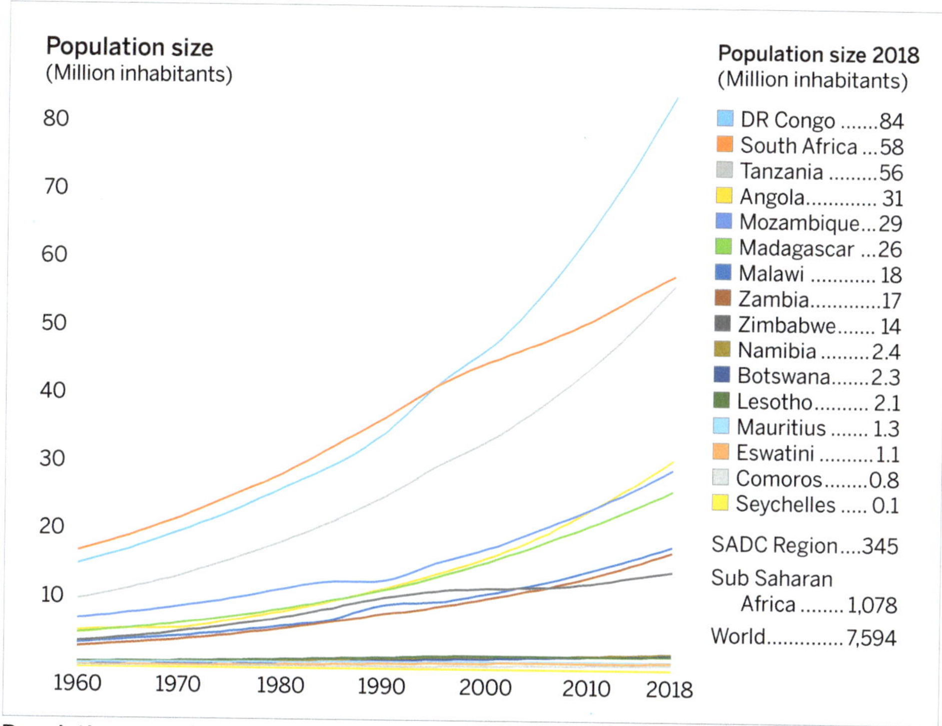

Population growth from 1960 to 2018. All 16 countries that are today SADC members. The data is based on the de facto definition of population, counting all residents regardless of legal status or citizenship. Data source: World Bank.

pasture and livestock in many SADC countries. Given the severe knock-on effects on food security, agricultural production and rural development, the SADC region is highly vulnerable to the adverse repercussions of extreme weather phenomena, whose frequency is likely to increase further owing to climate change.[53]

In sum, over the past three decades, Southern Africa has evolved from being one of the most war-riven to one of the most peaceful parts of Africa, as only a handful of isolated and comparatively low-intensity armed conflicts now affect the region. Most contemporary crises and security challenges, as the subsequent discussion of contemporary intrastate conflicts will underline, relate to deficits of governance and democracy, including electoral disputes, the unconstitutional change or retention of executive power, and the misappropriation or mismanagement of state resources by unaccountable governments. These risks to peace and security in the SADC region are compounded by challenges of socio-economic development. These challenges, which give rise to social unrest and undermine human security, result from both the economic legacies of settler colonialism and the inability of post-liberation governments to effectively tackle the tremendous social inequities and to enable the economic stimulation of a young and growing population in an adverse macroeconomic environment.

53 SADC, SADC Regional Vulnerability Assessment, pp. 9–13.

SADC Headquarters in Gaborone, Botswana, November 2017. Maite Nkoana-Mashabane, South Africa's minister of international relations and cooperation, and Stergomena Lawrence Tax, executive secretary of SADC, discuss the political situation in Zimbabwe after the coup d'état against Mugabe, at a meeting of the SADC troika plus council chair. Photo: DIRCO.

> The anti-imperialist defence reaction and solidarity has prevented the effective protection of human security by SADC.

Chapter 3, page 40

3. The development of SADC's institutional framework and policies on regional peace and security

SADC's predecessors and their institutional legacies

SADC's peace and security architecture and policies have been shaped by the institutional legacies of its predecessors, the dynamics among its heterogeneous membership, and the international standards set by the UN, the AU and the international donor community. SADC and, in particular, its Organ for Politics, Defence and Security emerged from the Frontline States (FLS), a defensive alliance of Southern African states which, alongside the Liberation Committee of the Organisation of African Unity (OAU), served the objective of coordinating the struggle against white minority rule in the region. After the presidents of Tanzania and Zambia had already formed the Mulungushi Club for the same purpose, the FLS was called into being in 1975, after the Lusophone states gained independence, and it came to play a vital role in supporting the Zimbabwean African nationalist movements during the war of liberation against the Rhodesian regime. The FLS, whose initial membership comprised Angola, Botswana, Lesotho, Mozambique, Swaziland, Tanzania and Zambia, was joined by Zimbabwe and Namibia after those countries' independence in 1980 and 1990, respectively.[54] Although the FLS leaders shared the common goal of ending white minority rule and developed strong personal ties, a sense of solidarity and – to some extent – a common regional identity, the relationship between the various liberation movements, which had different sponsors in the Cold War, and their governments was hardly without friction.[55]

SADC's second institutional predecessor, the Southern African Development Coordination Conference (SADCC), was formed in 1980, following the independence of Zimbabwe, whose government promptly took on a key role in the organisation. Like the FLS, SADCC served to develop a common response to the threats posed by the apartheid regime. But in contrast to the security-oriented FLS, the new regional organisation laid greater stress on economic cooperation to reduce the region's economic dependence on South Africa and its vulnerability to Pretoria's destabilisation tactics. The SADCC leaders articulated common positions on maintaining donor relations,

54 Khadiagala, 'The SADCC and its approaches', pp. 26, 35; Mlambo, Alois S., 'The Zimbabwean crisis and international response', Journal for Contemporary History, 31 (2006), p. 65.

55 Chung, Fay, Re-Living the Second Chimurenga: Memories from the liberation struggle in Zimbabwe (Harare, Weaver Press, 2006), pp. 123, 246; Mtisi et al., 'War in Rhodesia', p. 165; Southern African Liaison Office, South Africa's Relations with Zimbabwe: Pre-colonial to 2006 (Cape Town, 2013), pp. 64, 103; Van Nieuwkerk, 'The strategic culture', p. 54.

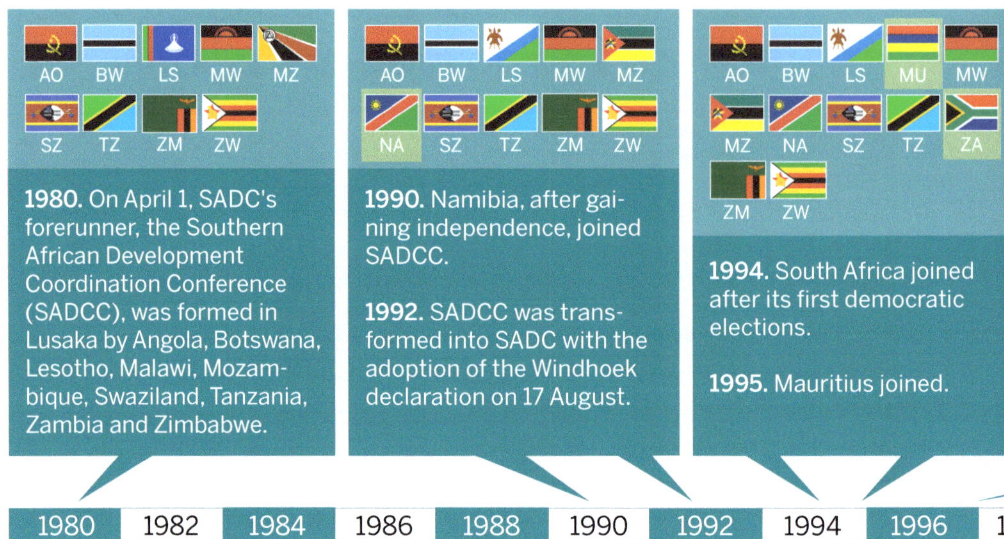

SADC's second predecessor, the Frontline States (FLS) alliance against apartheid, was formed in 1975 by Angola, Botswana, Mozambique, Tanzania and Zambia and in 1980 joined by Zimbabwe. FLS co-existed with SADCC until it was turned into the SADC Organ and merged into SADC in about 1996

condemning apartheid, supporting decolonisation and preparing for a liberated South Africa.[56] Emerging from these two organisations, SADC – which came into existence in 1992, when South Africa had not yet completed its democratic transition and was therefore ineligible to join the Community – ended up with a two-pronged structural setup, with the dual objectives of an economic community and a defensive alliance.[57] As will be explained in more detail below, a further lasting legacy of the two institutional predecessors consists in the preoccupation with the defence of national sovereignty against outside interference and the anti-imperialist outlook that is reflected in SADC's approach to managing conflicts and security in the region.

The development of SADC's institutional framework

The constitutive SADC Treaty established the Summit of SADC Heads of State and Government as the highest policy- and decision-making body. As extraordinary summits are frequently required to address pressing matters, the SADC heads of state convene at least twice a year. The SADC Summit is hosted by a rotating SADC Chair,

56 Khadiagala, 'The SADCC and its approaches', p. 26; Van Nieuwkerk, 'The strategic culture', p. 61; Nyakudya, Munyaradzi, 'SADC's crisis management in Zimbabwe, 2007–2013', in Anthoni Van Nieuwkerk and Katharina Hofmann (eds), Southern African Security Review 2013 (Maputo, Friedrich Ebert Stiftung, 2013, p. 85; Tjønneland, Elling N., 'Making sense of the Southern African Development Community', African Security Review, 22, 3 (2013), p. 192.

57 Nathan, Community of Insecurity, p. 23.

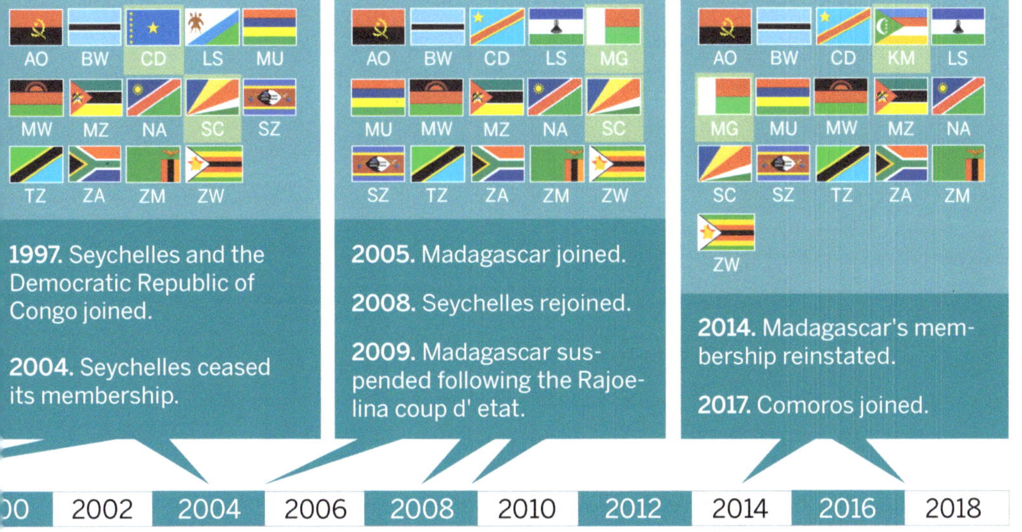

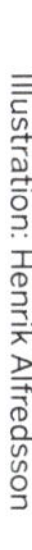

who is confirmed by the heads of state on an annual basis. The presiding, previous and succeeding SADC chairs form the SADC Troika, which fulfils a coordinating function and occasionally meets to address urgent concerns and to make recommendations that, however, must be approved by the Summit.[58] Resolutions by the Summit and other SADC bodies require a quorum and two-thirds majority, but Summit decisions are expected to be made consensually and to be binding. While the Summit's regular meetings serve to provide resolutions on policies concerned with economic integration and political matters, the Summit serves equally as the highest decision-making body for resolving matters of regional peace and security.[59] In its original structural setup, SADC's institutional framework did not include a forum dedicated to peace and security, other than the Summit, and nor was there a ministerial committee to develop the regional peace and security architecture.[60]

SADC's second-highest political decision-making body is the Council of Ministers, which consists of the member states' foreign ministers. The Council advises the Summit and oversees the development and implementation of SADC policies, as well as the overall functioning of the organisation. It also superintends the Integrated Committee of Ministers, which is appointed by member states to monitor joint activities relating to trade, industry, finance, investment, infrastructure, food and agriculture, natural resources and social development.[61]

58 Hendricks, Cheryl and Musavengana, Takawira (eds), The Security Sector in Southern Africa (Pretoria, Institute for Security Studies, 2010), p. 16; International Crisis Group (ICG), Implementing Peace and Security Architecture (II): Southern Africa (Johannesburg, 2012), p 1.

59 Van Nieuwkerk, 'The strategic culture', p. 55.

60 Nathan, Community of Insecurity, pp. 23–27.

61 ICG, Implementing Peace, p. 1; Nathan, Community of Insecurity, p. 23.

Due both to the reluctance of member states to establish supranational structures and to their limited resources, SADC's decision-making organs are only supported by a small and insufficiently resourced Secretariat, which is based in Gaborone. Consequently, the implementation of SADC policies relies heavily on the bureaucratic structures and resources of the member states. The SADC Secretariat has a series of directorates dedicated to specific policy domains, including a Directorate for Politics, Defence and Security, which supports the Organ. The SADC Secretariat is directed by the Executive Secretary, who is elected by the Summit and who, in the past, has taken on a central role in effecting diplomatic initiatives in the domain of peace and security.[62] The present Executive Secretary, Stergomena Lawrence Tax of Tanzania, assumed office in August 2013.[63]

Under the Treaty, SADC established a Parliamentary Forum in 1996; in principle, its mandate is to promote peace, security and stability, as well as human rights and democracy in the region. The SADC Parliamentary Forum has been most visible through its involvement in election observation missions, as well as through the promotion of electoral standards and the parliamentary representation of women. It can also review the annual reports of the Secretariat and make recommendations on the SADC budget. However, the status of the Parliamentary Forum is unclear, and it fulfils neither a legislative nor an effective oversight function. Although SADC's founding documents suggest that the Forum should become a fully functional supranational legislature, member states are unwilling to transfer legislative power from national parliaments to SADC. Since coming into existence, the Parliamentary Forum has been virtually absent from the policy-making process and has been excluded from the development of security policies and Organ activities. Consequently, it primarily serves as a forum for the members of national parliaments to exchange views and experiences.[64]

By contrast, the Windhoek-based SADC Tribunal – inaugurated in 2005 – swiftly became a fully functional supranational court of justice, ruling on member states' compliance with SADC's legal framework. The Tribunal's existence was, however, short lived: in 2007, following a petition by a group of white farmers who had been dispossessed during Zimbabwe's fast-track land-reform programme, the Tribunal ruled that the constitutional amendment legalising the land reform violated the SADC Treaty; that the reform, whose terms it deemed arbitrary, amounted to racial discrimination as it targeted only white farmers; and that the Zimbabwean state should compensate the farmers for the land expropriated. The Zimbabwean government ignored the verdict, and in 2009 announced that it would withdraw from the Tribunal's jurisdiction, arguing that its rulings were null and void, as the Tribunal's protocol had not been ratified by a two-thirds majority. After Zimbabwe lobbied the region, SADC's 2010 Annual Summit decided

---

62 Cawthra, Gavin, The Role of SADC in Managing Political Crisis and Conflict: The cases of Madagascar and Zimbabwe (Maputo, Friedrich Ebert Stiftung, 2011), p. 11; Tjønneland, 'Making sense of the Southern African Development Community', p. 169.

63 SADC, Summit Communiqué, Lilongwe, 18.8.13.

64 Hendricks and Musavengana, The Security Sector in Southern Africa, pp. 31–33; ICG, Implementing Peace, p. 7.

to review the Tribunal's role, functions and terms of reference.[65] Although, in 2011, an independent review commissioned by the Secretariat reaffirmed the legal basis and all the verdicts of the Tribunal, the Summit failed to reappoint the members of the Tribunal, thus effectively suspending the court of law that is enshrined in the SADC Treaty.[66]

A year later, the Summit resolved that a new protocol on the Tribunal should be negotiated; this would confine its mandate to interpretation of the SADC Treaty and Protocols as they relate to disputes between member states.[67] Following a report from the Committee of Ministers of Justice, in 2014 the Summit adopted a new protocol on the SADC Tribunal, which would henceforth only be allowed to accept cases referred by states, and not by citizens. A year later, the heads of state resolved to establish a disempowered SADC Administrative Tribunal (SADCAT).[68] However, only nine states, including Zimbabwe, signed the new protocol; the remaining six would not do so, owing to concerns over the Tribunal's constrained terms of reference and potential conflicts with the SADC Treaty. By 2016, the protocol had still not been approved by all members. Thus, at the time of writing, the supranational Tribunal that SADC resolved to establish under its 1992 Treaty has yet to be reinstated.[69]

By curtailing its powers and indefinitely suspending the SADC Tribunal, the Summit dismantled a vital conflict-resolution mechanism and democratic institution that was designed to protect SADC's founding principles and citizens' rights against despotic regimes that had co-opted their respective national judiciary. The resolution of the overwhelmingly powerful Summit to scrap the regional court of law the moment it reached an inconvenient verdict caused both tremendous institutional and reputational damage, for it not only illustrated SADC's institutional weakness, but also exposed the member states' lack of commitment to principles of constitutional democracy, and their unwillingness to relinquish sovereign power to supranational structures.[70]

The 'Implantation' of the Organ for Politics, Defence and Security into SADC

The Organ for Politics, Defence and Security – which, alongside the Summit, constitutes the most important SADC institution to manage regional peace and security – came into existence in 1996 as the FLS's successor, but without being fully integrated into SADC's

65 For a detailed discussion of the case and Tribunal's suspension, see: Nathan, Laurie, 'Solidarity triumphs over democracy – the dissolution of the SADC Tribunal', Development Dialogue, 57 (2011), pp.125–29; SADC, 30th Jubilee Ordinary Summit Communiqué, Windhoek, 20.8.10, Para 32.

66 Nathan, 'Solidarity triumphs', p. 131; SADC, Extraordinary Summit Communiqué, Windhoek, 20.5.11. Paras 7–8.

67 SADC, 32nd Summit Communiqué, Maputo, 18.8.12, Para 24.

68 SADC, 34th Summit Communiqué, Victoria Falls, 18.8.14; SADC, 35th Summit Communiqué, Gaborone, 18.8.17.

69 Veritas, The Protocol on the SADC Tribunal, Bill Watch 24/2014, Harare, 10.11.14; SADC, 36th Summit Communiqué, Mbabane, 31.8.16.

70 Aeby, 'Zimbabwe's gruelling transition', p. 272.

institutional framework. While Zimbabwe, whose president, Robert Mugabe, chaired the Organ, wanted it to remain a separate organisation, South Africa sought to subject the Organ to the authority of the SADC Summit. For the first five years of its existence, as Laurie Nathan highlights, the Organ, which lacked a protocol to give it a legal basis, operated as a competitor to the SADC Summit; this resulted in a situation where two forums of heads of state made decisions concerning matters of regional peace and security.[71] According to Matlosa, the region failed to respond to multiple conflict situations during this period because of the protracted dispute over the status of the Organ.[72]

While drafting started two years earlier, the heads of state could only agree on a protocol for the Organ at the 2001 Annual Summit, when Mugabe – whose government was in a deep crisis of legitimacy and faced a standoff with Western donor nations – was compelled to relinquish chairmanship of the Organ.[73] Under the Protocol on Politics, Defence and Security Cooperation, the Organ, whose overall objective is to promote peace and security, shall:

- safeguard the people and development of the region against instability arising from the breakdown of law and order, intra- and interstate conflict and aggression;
- promote political cooperation, common values and institutions;
- develop common foreign policies that are to be advocated in international forums;
- coordinate regional security and defence;
- prevent intra- and inter-state conflict by peaceful means and consider enforcement where peaceful means do not suffice;
- promote democratic institutions and universal human rights;
- encourage member states to implement AU and UN treaties on arms control and disarmament; and
- enhance regional capacity for peace-keeping, disaster management and the coordination of international humanitarian assistance.[74]

Combining the promotion of peace and security with democracy and human rights, as well as development and humanitarian concerns, the 2001 Protocol thus reflects to some extent the liberal peace and human security agenda advanced by the UN since the middle of the 1990s. By mandating the Organ to respond to intrastate conflicts, the Protocol also indicated a shift from a Westphalian conception of sovereignty toward the doctrine of Responsibility to Protect; this would also be reflected in the Constitutive Act of the African Union, which replaced the OAU a year later.[75] In prac-

71 Nathan, Community of Insecurity, pp. 38–42.
72 Matlosa, 'Elections and conflict management', p. 115.
73 Kagwanja, Peter, 'Power and peace: South Africa and the refurbishing of Africa's multilateral capacity for peacemaking', in R. Southall (ed.), South Africa's Role in Conflict Resolution and Peacemaking in Africa (Cape Town, HSRC Press, 2006), p. 35.
74 SADC, Protocol on Politics, Defence and Security Cooperation, Blantyre, 14.8.01, Art. 1.
75 Constitutive Act of the African Union, 2002, Art. 3–4.

tice, however, SADC leaders have frequently prioritised national sovereignty over the protection of the citizenry from arbitrary rule.

Under the Protocol, the 'methods employed by the Organ to prevent, manage and resolve conflict by peaceful means shall include preventive diplomacy, negotiations, conciliation, mediation, good offices, arbitration and adjudication by an international tribunal'.[76] As Nathan highlights, since the Summit obliged the Organ to rely primarily on peaceful means to resolve crises, a pacific group of SADC states led by South Africa prevailed over the militarist camp, represented by Zimbabwe. The pacific group, however, conceded that the Organ would develop a Mutual Defence Pact; this was adopted in 2003 and obliges SADC to take collective action in response to an attack on a member state.[77]

Given Mugabe's long-standing grip on the chairmanship and his controversial decisions during his tenure, SADC leaders were anxious to avoid any overt concentration of power in the hands of one head of state. The Protocol, therefore, stipulates that the Organ is subordinate to the Summit and is headed by a Troika, whose chair cannot simultaneously hold the chairmanship of the SADC Summit.[78] The Organ chair, in consultation with the Organ Troika, which functions as a steering committee, is responsible for the policy objectives and crisis interventions of the Organ during a one-year tenure. A Ministerial Committee of the Organ (comprising the ministers of foreign affairs, defence, public security and state security of each state) coordinates the work of the Organ structures. The foreign and security ministers, moreover, form an Inter-state Politics and Diplomacy Committee (ISPDC) and an Inter-State Defence and Security Committee (ISDSC), respectively; these convene at least once a year to coordinate policies on joint security.[79] A Directorate for Politics, Defence and Security Affairs, based at the SADC Secretariat in Gaborone, supports the Organ in terms of administration, strategic planning, policy development, implementation and monitoring.[80] In practice, the small directorate has thus far played a minor role in conflict management, due to its limited organisational capacity.[81]

As Hendricks and Musavengana emphasise, the integration of the Organ into the SADC structure markedly improved governance of the security sector after the previous FLS arrangements, and reduced the risk of contentious troop deployments, as during the Second Congo War. As they argued in their 2010 analysis, though there is a degree of transparency surrounding the work of the Organ, the decision-making processes are still not transparent to the public, and SADC's engagement with civil society on security matters is very limited.[82] That assessment remains valid at the time of writing.

---

76 SADC, Protocol on Politics, Defence and Security Cooperation, Blantyre, 14.8.01, Art. 10.

77 Nathan, Community of Insecurity, pp. 46, 57.

78 Nathan, Community of Insecurity, p. 46.

79 Hendricks and Musavengana, The Security Sector in Southern Africa, p. 16.

80 Van Nieuwkerk, 'The strategic culture', p. 55.

81 Tjønneland, 'Making sense of the Southern African Development Community', p. 139; Cawthra, The Role of SADC, p. 11.

82 Hendricks and Musavengana, The Security Sector in Southern Africa, p. 16.

The implementation of the Strategic Indicative Plan for the Organ

In 2002, the Summit mandated the Organ and its Directorate to develop a Strategic Indicative Plan for the Organ (SIPO) that was meant to operationalise the corresponding Protocol by drawing up guidelines and an institutional framework for the Organ's activities.[83] Moreover, SIPO was supposed to align SADC's peace and security agenda with that of the AU, which came into being the same year. SIPO and its peace and security provisions were not conceived as an end in themselves, but as a means of creating a peaceful environment to achieve implementation of SADC's Regional Indicative Strategic Development Plan (RISDP).[84] By linking security to human development and the RISDP, SIPO thus marked a further step towards the adoption of a human security approach.[85]

SIPO identified key challenges and set out vaguely defined, repetitive and overlapping strategies and activities in four sectors: politics, defence, state security and public security. In the political domain, key challenges included underdevelopment; HIV/AIDS; intra- and interstate conflict; democracy and governance; migration; inequitable access to resources; natural disasters; and corruption. These were meant to be tackled through the exchange of information, diplomatic initiatives, the promotion of socio-economic development, bilateral commissions and greater regional cooperation. Moreover, SIPO envisaged regular risk assessments, early warning and greater conflict prevention capacity; common electoral standards and commissions for elections and human rights; enhanced coordination on peace-keeping and disaster management; and the operationalisation of the Inter-state Politics and Diplomacy Committee.[86]

In the defence sector, SIPO identified as key challenges armed intrastate conflicts; terrorism; the capacity to support peace operations and provide disaster relief; defence technology; landmines; external aggression; arms proliferation; and demobilisation, disarmament and reintegration (DDR). SIPO aimed at addressing these challenges through an overall harmonisation of national defence policies, including the finalisation of the Mutual Defence Pact, greater interaction between state security and defence forces, the development of regional defence capacity against aggression, a standby arrangement for peace operations, and the promotion of civilian-military relations.[87]

With respect to state security, the authors of SIPO saw the greatest challenges in internally and externally induced threats and manoeuvres to subvert constitutional order, diminish national sovereignty and damage the economic interests of SADC states. To enhance the region's preventive capacity against these threats, SIPO envisaged impro-

83 Nathan, Community of Insecurity, p. 52.

84 Arthur, Peter, 'Promoting security in Africa through regional economic communities (RECs) and the African Union's African Peace and Security Architecture (APSA)', Insight on Africa, 9, 1 (2017), p. 7; Van Nieuwkerk, 'Exploring', p. 42.

85 Zondi, Siphamandla, 'Comprehensive and holistic human security for a post-colonial Southern Africa: A conceptual framework', Strategic Review for Southern Africa, 39, 1 (2017), p. 197.

86 SADC, Strategic Indicative Plan for the Organ for Politics, Defence and Security Cooperation, Gaborone, 2002, pp. 15–22.

87 SADC, Strategic Indicative Plan for the Organ, 2002, pp. 23–29.

ving intelligence cooperation and training programmes, establishing an early warning system in line with the APSA framework, and protecting maritime resources.[88]

Finally, in terms of public security, SIPO highlighted transnational, organised and violent crime as a key challenge that may involve cyber-crime, terrorism, drugs and arms trafficking, financial crime, human trafficking, sexual violence and trade in conflict minerals. These were to be tackled by greater information sharing through databases; harmonised immigration procedures; improved training and a joint code of conduct; and a culture of human rights for law-enforcement agencies, community policing, disaster management coordination, and regular evaluations.[89]

In sum, SIPO resembled a declaration of intent, rather than a coherent and elaborate policy blueprint to operationalise the Organ's Protocol in pursuit of its objectives. The realisation of SADC's peace and security objectives would, therefore, require extensive policy development, for which the Organ (and its under-resourced directorate) were poorly equipped. Notwithstanding these shortcomings, SIPO constituted a considerable step towards more concerted management of a much broader catalogue of common peace and security concerns of SADC member states.[90]

Although initially planned for a five-year period, SIPO remained the Organ's guiding document until 2012, when it was replaced by SIPO II. In his analysis of the implementation of SIPO, Van Nieuwkerk regards the major achievements of the 10 years of the Plan as including the conclusion of the Mutual Defence Pact, the launch of the SADC Standby Force, the integration of the Southern African Regional Police Chiefs Cooperation into the ISDSC, and the creation of the Regional Early Warning Centre and the SADC Electoral Advisory Council. However, he observes that SIPO was poorly implemented in many regards. The relevant SADC institutions failed to produce a business plan to realise SIPO's objectives; to develop serious strategies to operationalise the Organ; and (as will be discussed below) to harmonise SADC's peace and security architecture with the APSA in a timely manner.[91] The implementation backlog covered shortcomings in terms of programme design and management, appropriate structures, staffing and financial resources, monitoring and evaluation procedures, as well as political control, donor policies and contextual factors, such as conflict-prone environments.[92]

SIPO II was adopted by the Summit in 2010, after a review that year of the much-criticised first plan; however, it only came into effect two years later. Like its predecessor, SIPO II was developed by security officials with little outside assistance or civil society input, although the Organ received technical support from the German Development Agency, and a number of Southern African think tanks were willing to provide expertise.[93] SIPO II differs from its predecessor in that it includes the police as a fifth sector,

88 SADC, Strategic Indicative Plan for the Organ, 2002, pp. 30–34.
89 SADC, Strategic Indicative Plan for the Organ, 2002, pp. 35–42.
90 Van Nieuwkerk and Notshulwana, 'A critical examination', p. 26.
91 Van Nieuwkerk and Notshulwana, 'A critical examination', p. 26.
92 Van Nieuwkerk and Notshulwana, 'A critical examination', p. 26.
93 Van Nieuwkerk, 'The strategic culture', p. 63; Van Nieuwkerk, Anthoni, "SIPO II: Too little, too late?', Strategic Review for Southern Africa, 35 (9 June 2013), p. 149.

alongside defence, political, state and public security. While the challenges and strategies listed in the first four sectors largely replicate the content of the original SIPO, the revised Plan provides more detail about activities to achieve the objectives set for each sector, though without determining who should carry out the activities. SIPO II identifies additional threats (such as piracy), places greater emphasis on civilian participation in conflict transformation, and devotes considerably more attention to monitoring and evaluation. The challenges that it identifies for the police sector mirror those pertaining to state security. SIPO II stresses the responsibility of police to crack down on transnational crime, which is to be achieved through the development of joint crime management strategies, information management, training and cooperation with Interpol.[94] Overall, SIPO II provides a mechanical, overlapping and repetitive sectoral analysis that, according to Van Nieuwkerk, was already dated when the plan came into effect in 2012. The revised plan stresses the need for policy harmonisation, but does not offer any guidelines for joint foreign and security policy development processes. While SADC officials consider SIPO II to be a guide for collective action, rather than a legally binding policy blueprint, the Organ lacks an integrated and elaborate business plan to realise its objectives.[95] The initial lifespan of SIPO II came to an end in 2015, but it was extended to 2020 after an internal evaluation undertaken in 2016.[96]

At the time of writing, no comprehensive and systematic independent analysis of the implementation of SIPO II has been undertaken. In an expert interview conducted for this study, Anthoni van Nieuwkerk highlights some achievements by SADC member states with regard to the implementation process. First, some progress has been made in terms of the pursuit of democracy and stability through improved election management and democracy promotion. Secondly, the establishment of a comprehensive mediation and conflict management architecture in line with the APSA (as will be discussed shortly) has somewhat strengthened SADC's ability to undertake peace-making and peace-keeping in a coordinated manner. Thirdly, SADC's ability to pursue robust peace-keeping missions has also been enhanced by the improved readiness of the SADC Standby Force and political will to deploy these troops. Fourthly, the development of an early warning system, alongside other activities in the state security sector, has improved the region's ability to respond to threats to peace and security. Finally, better police cooperation and coordination among SADC states has improved the management of public safety and crime fighting.[97]

Impediments to the implementation of SIPO II and achievement of its goals relate primarily to the availability and allocation by member states of tangible and intangible resources for the implementation of the plan. The relevant SADC institutions must develop greater capacity for implementation and evaluation, which would require the employment of well-trained officials across the organisation. Improved coordination

94 Van Nieuwkerk, 'Exploring', p. 46; SADC, Revised Edition of the Strategic Indicative Plan for the Organ, Maputo, 2010, pp. 23–53.

95 Van Nieuwkerk, 'Exploring', p. 47; Van Nieuwkerk, SIPO II, p. 150.

96 Anthoni Van Nieuwkerk, interview via email, Johannesburg, 12.12.17.

97 Anthoni Van Nieuwkerk, interview via email, Johannesburg, 12.12.17.

both within SADC (i.e. between the Secretariat and other supranational institutions) and between SADC and its 16 member states constitutes a further challenge.[98] As Nathan points out, the lack of resources and political support for the newly established structures is due to the fact that the creation of these peace and security institutions was a response to SADC's obligation vis-à-vis the AU to operationalise the APSA, and was driven by the small Secretariat and donors, rather than by member states. Some SADC states, meanwhile, lack genuine commitment to the development of the supranational institutional framework for peace and security in the region, as they are unwilling to cede authority and resources to SADC.[99] Critical SADC structures, including the mediation infrastructure, are also starved of resources, as the use of donor funds in the sensitive domain of peace and security is highly problematic, on account of the risk of donor influence. SADC states are, however, more willing to accept donor funding for the training and deployment of peace-keepers. With well over half of its budget financed by international donors, rather than member states, SADC is vulnerable to undue influence from (mostly) Western donor nations.[100]

The operationalisation of SADC's APSA component

A major driver of the institutional development of SADC's peace and security architecture and a SIPO objective is the integration of SADC into the APSA, whose structures are enshrined in the 2002 Protocol Relating to the Establishment of the Peace and Security Council of the African Union. As with other regional economic communities (RECs), this has required the creation of structures at the SADC level that feed into the AU's principal APSA components: the Peace and Security Council; Panel of the Wise; African Standby Force; Continental Early Warning System; and Peace Fund.[101] The development of the relevant SADC institutions has long lagged behind schedule. Although the SADC brigade has fared well, compared to the troop contingents of other RECs, the establishment of the SADC Standby Force was delayed, as questions of coordination and authority for troop deployments remained unanswered.[102]

During the lifespan of SIPO II, substantial progress has been made in terms of strengthening the capacity of the Standby Force's planning element, which comprises military, police and civilian components. The SADC Standby Force's readiness for deployment was demonstrated by the UN-mandated Force Intervention Brigade in

98 Anthoni Van Nieuwkerk, interview via email, Johannesburg, 12.12.17.

99 Laurie Nathan, interview via email, 2.12.17.

100 Cawthra, Gavin, 'The role of donors and NGOs in the security policy process in southern Africa', in A. Van Nieuwkerk and K. Hofmann (eds), Southern African Security Review 2013 (Maputo, Friedrich Ebert Stiftung, 2013), pp. 28–32; Nathan, Community of Insecurity, p. 134.

101 Tieku, Thomas Kwasi, Obi, Cyril and Scorgie-Porter, Lindsay, 'The African Peace and Security Architecture: Introduction to the special issue', African Conflict and Peacebuilding Review, 4, 2 (2014), pp. 1–10; Williams Paul D., 'Reflections on the evolving African Peace and Security Architecture', African Security, 7, 3 (2014), pp. 147–62; Arthur, 'Promoting security', p. 10.

102 Cawthra, The Role of SADC, p. 11; Van Nieuwkerk, SIPO II, p. 147.

the DRC (with troops drawn from SADC states) and by a troop contingent sent to Lesotho to ensure stability while mediation efforts were under way. There was delay, however, in the establishment of an Operations Centre for the Standby Force, intended to improve communication and coordination of operations with field missions and the AU.[103] Like the standby forces of other RECs, the SADC troops continued to encounter challenges relating to inadequate human resources, logistics and the need to refine decision-making processes surrounding the integrated planning of missions by Standby Force components.[104] To strengthen these capabilities, SADC runs a Regional Peace-keeping Training Centre in Harare that is co-funded by international donors.[105]

In the pivotal domain of conflict prevention and peace-making, SADC has established a Regional Early Warning System, a Mediation Reference Group, a Panel of Elders and a Mediation Support Unit. These are supposed to provide information to the corresponding continental institutions and to give technical support to SADC missions to prevent and manage conflicts. However, a lack of political and financial support means that these structures that can significantly improve the quality of SADC's most important conflict management strategy – mediation – have thus far not lived up to their full potential.[106] At the time of writing, mediation support needs to be improved through increased capacities for research, analysis and information dissemination. Although the SADC mediation structures provide a suitable platform, member states involved in mediation missions do not sufficiently coordinate their diplomatic efforts with the Secretariat and the mediation structures as a whole. In theory, early warning and mediation are linked, so as to enable preventive diplomacy; but this is not the case in practice. The coordination of the Regional Early Warning System and the Mediation Support Unit, therefore, requires further work. The ability to monitor, evaluate and ensure the implementation of agreements brokered by SADC mediators and guaranteed by the Summit is equally limited.[107] Moreover, SADC's state-centred peace initiatives, which rely heavily on high-level mediation, fall short in terms of the inclusion of women and civil society actors.[108]

---

103 Cawthra, The Role of SADC, p. 11; Hendricks and Musavengana, The Security Sector in Southern Africa, pp. 20–24; Anthoni Van Nieuwkerk, interview via email, Johannesburg, 12.12.17; Laurie Nathan, interview via email, 2.12.17.

104 Cawthra, The Role of SADC, p. 11; Hendricks and Musavengana, The Security Sector in Southern Africa, pp. 20–24; Anthoni Van Nieuwkerk, interview via email, Johannesburg, 12.12.17; Laurie Nathan, interview via email, 2.12.17.

105 Cawthra, 'The role of donors', p. 32.

106 Laurie Nathan, interview via email, 2.12.17.

107 Anthoni Van Nieuwkerk, interview via email, Johannesburg, 12.12.17.

108 Aeby, Michael, 'Making an impact from the margins? Civil society groups in Zimbabwe's interim power-sharing process', Journal of Modern African Studies, 54, 4 (2016), pp. 712–14; Anthoni Van Nieuwkerk, interview via email, Johannesburg, 12.12.17.

Regional dynamics and norms informing SADC's conflict management in practice

SADC's founding documents and policy plans, alongside those of the AU, contain normative standards and guidelines for the organisation's conflict management. They establish a strong link between peace and security, on the one hand, and democracy, on the other. In practice, however, a different set of norms applies, and the principle of the sovereignty of national executives (which is also enshrined in the two organisations' constitutive treaties) takes precedence.[109] Under the SADC Treaty, the Guidelines Governing Democratic Elections and the Protocol of the Organ, SADC is supposed to promote peace and security, stability and development, democratic institutions and governance, the rule of law, respect for human rights, and equity and solidarity in the region. Although they aim at regional integration and collective security arrangements to respond to inter- and intrastate conflicts, these documents equally stress respect for national sovereignty.[110] The Constitutive Act of the AU, the African Charter on Democracy, Elections and Governance, and the African Charter on Human and Peoples' Rights provide similar normative guidelines. The AU's founding principles rule out the unconstitutional change of government and retention of state power. While upholding the right to self-determination and trumpeting defence of national sovereignty as one of the organisation's purposes, AU treaties explicitly provide for humanitarian interventions and diplomatic missions to safeguard democracy.[111] Tensions between conflicting norms are, thus, already inherent in the regional and continental peace and security policy framework.

In practice, the principles that are applied in response to recurring intrastate crises are repeatedly renegotiated by the heterogeneous membership of SADC, where stability and sovereignty tend to take precedence over democracy for a number of reasons. SADC's capability for enforcing its democratic founding principles in states that violate the SADC Treaty and the other documents mentioned above are severely limited. Strict enforcement in cases where authoritarian regimes hold onto power by undemocratic and violent means runs the risk of further undermining stability, as was the case in Zimbabwe.[112] Moreover, since the spectrum of regime types in the region varies greatly, a number of member states lack genuine commitment to SADC's democratic principles, which were adopted in response to the hegemony of the liberal democratic discourse in international forums, dependence on international financial institutions and donors who insist on these standards, and the AU's democratic conventions.[113]

109 Aeby, 'Stability and sovereignty', p. 273; Nathan, Community of Insecurity, pp. 23–25.

110 SADC, Treaty, Chap. 3, Art. 4–5; SADC, Principles and Guidelines Governing Democratic Elections, 2004, Art. 2; SADC, Protocol on Politics, Art. 2.

111 AU, African Charter on Democracy, Elections and Governance, 2007, Art. 2–3; AU, Constitutive Act of the African Union, 2002, Arts. 3–4; Cole, Rowland J.V., 'Power-sharing, post-electoral contestations and the dismemberment of the right to democracy in Africa', International Journal of Human Rights, 17, 2 (2013), pp. 259–61.

112 Aeby, 'Stability and sovereignty', p. 273; Nathan, Community of Insecurity, p. 255.

113 Matlosa, 'Elections and conflict management', pp. 79–80; Nathan, 'Solidarity triumphs', p. 134.

According to SADC's former Executive Secretary, Simba Makoni, governments that lack commitment to such norms are unwilling to hold other member states to account, because they risk being subjected to the same discipline if they fail to comply with SADC principles.[114]

The most significant regional dynamic that continues to give direction to SADC's conflict management is the anti-imperialist doctrine and solidarity among liberation-party governments. Owing to their historical role in the struggle against colonialism and white minority rule, the governments of Angola, Mozambique, Namibia, Tanzania and Zimbabwe, alongside the economic hegemon South Africa, are highly respected in the circle of former liberation movements, and wield political influence in the region that is out of all proportion to their economic and military weight.[115] The solidarity of liberation-party governments stems from their common anti-imperialist ethos – which regards the parties as the custodians of social justice, transformation and national sovereignty – and the camaraderie of veteran leaders, who share the experience of racial oppression and the joint struggle against settler colonialism.[116] In the context of overt Western calls for regime change in Zimbabwe, military interventions to topple the regimes in Iraq, Côte d'Ivoire and Libya, and sustained efforts by embattled regimes to portray themselves as victims of a neo-colonial agenda, the solidarity of these African nationalist governments has prompted an anti-imperialist defensive reaction. As a result, democratic states such as South Africa and Namibia have acquiesced in the violation of democratic SADC principles, human rights abuses and corrupt maladministration by states like Zimbabwe which imperil the stability of the region, because democratic liberation-party governments equally give priority to the defence of African sovereignty against Western interference.[117] The anti-imperialist defence reaction and solidarity has prevented the effective protection of human security by SADC. According to Nathan, anti-imperialism is, however, the sole common value of SADC's heterogeneous and divided membership. In the absence of a canon of common values and norms, he argues, SADC is unable to become a genuine security community or to establish an effective security regime, notwithstanding the Southern African nations' shared interest in regional peace and security.[118]

114 Simba Makoni, interview, 15.3.13.

115 Laurie Nathan, interview via email, 2.12.17.

116 Simba Makoni, interview, 15.3.13; Melber, 'Southern African liberation movements', p. 454; Ndlovu-Gatsheni, Sabelo, 'Politics behind politics: African Union, SADC and the GPA in Zimbabwe', in B. Raftopoulos (ed.), The Hard Road to Reform (Harare, Weaver Press, 2013), p. 143.

117 Aeby, 'Zimbabwe's gruelling transition', pp. 156–60; International Crisis Group, Zimbabwe's Sanctions Standoff (Johannesburg, 2012), p. 1; Chikane, Frank, Eight Days in September: The removal of Thabo Mbeki (Johannesburg, Picador Africa, 2012), p. 96; Southern African Liaison Office, South Africa's Relations with Zimbabwe, p. 225; Sydney Mufamadi, interview, 14.3.14.

118 Nathan, Community of Insecurity, p. 70.

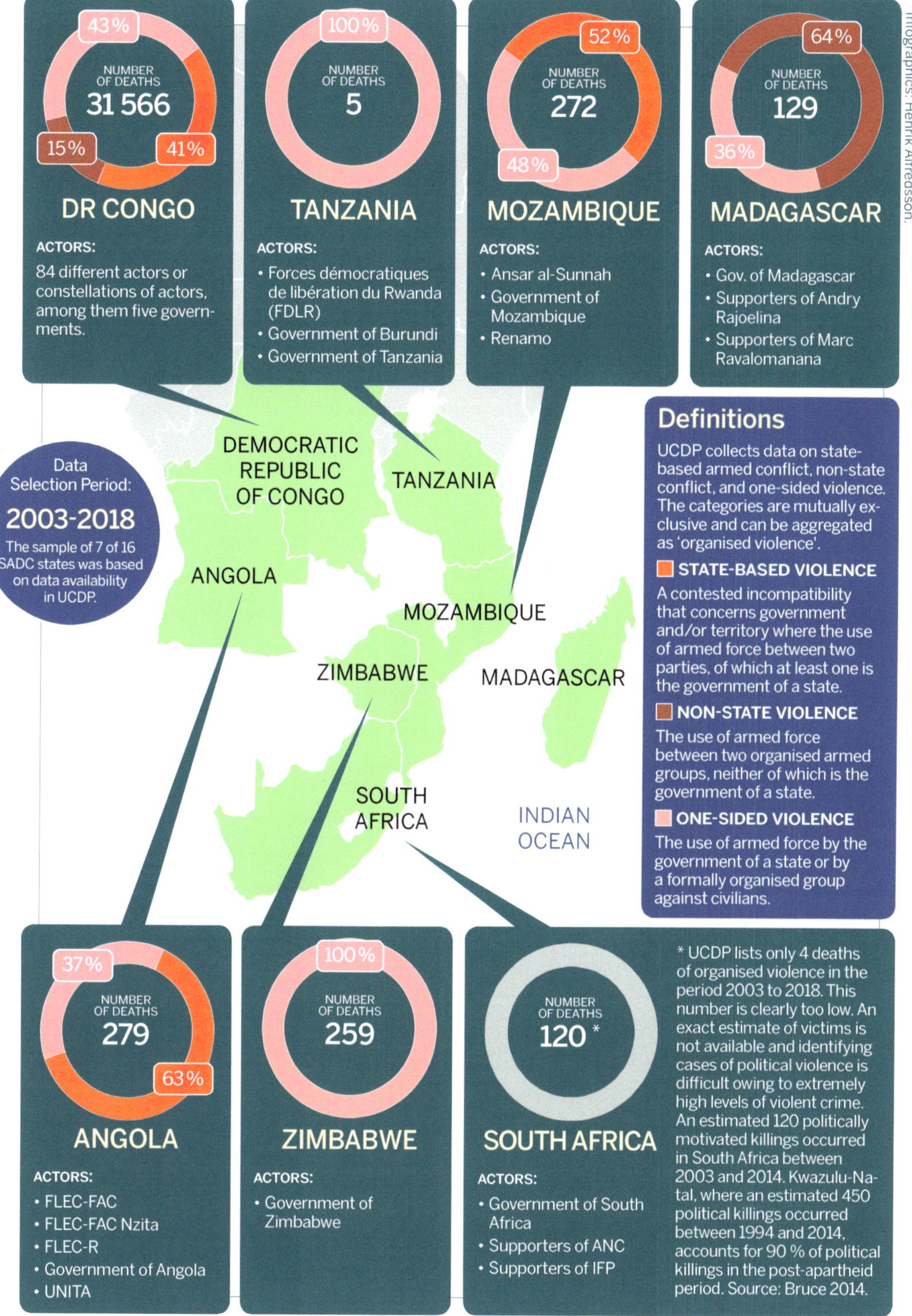

Number of deaths in organised violence in 7 of the 16 SADC countries from 2003 to 2018.
Source: Uppsala Conflict Data Program (UCDP), August 2019.

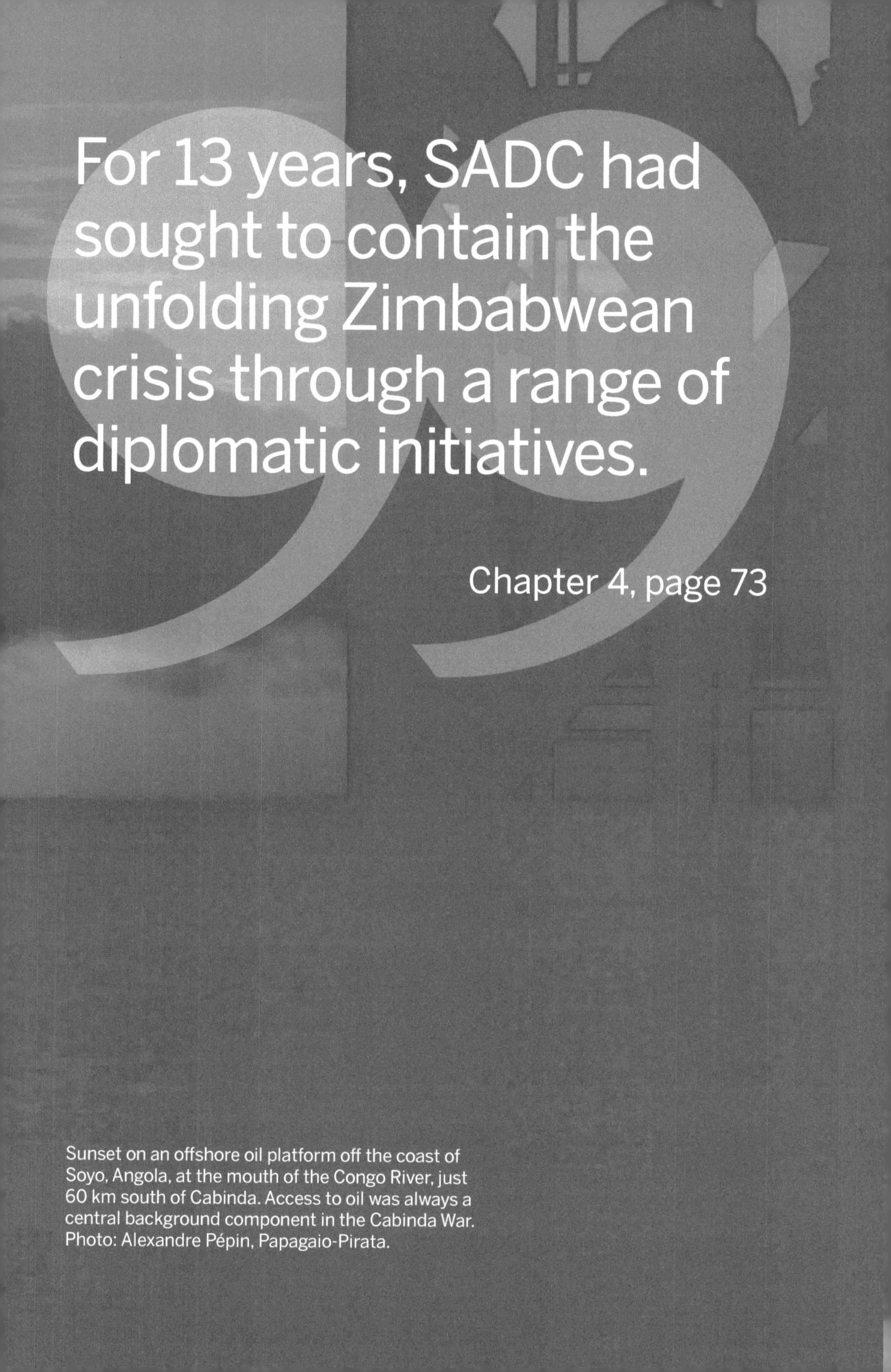

For 13 years, SADC had sought to contain the unfolding Zimbabwean crisis through a range of diplomatic initiatives.

Chapter 4, page 73

Sunset on an offshore oil platform off the coast of Soyo, Angola, at the mouth of the Congo River, just 60 km south of Cabinda. Access to oil was always a central background component in the Cabinda War. Photo: Alexandre Pépin, Papagaio-Pirata.

MOZAMBIQUE p. 45-51

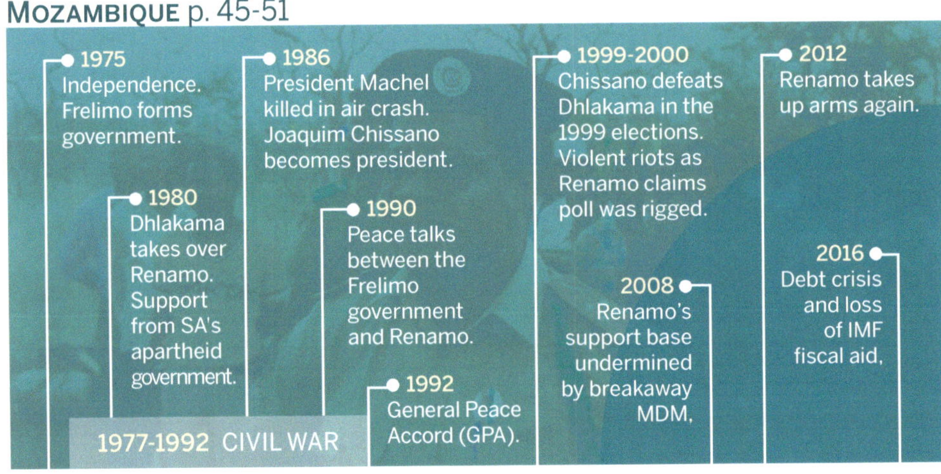

ANGOLA p. 51-57

1975 The Alvor Agreement ends the war for independence while marking the transition to the Civil War.

1979 MPLA leader Agostinho Neto dies. Jose Eduardo dos Santos takes over as president.

1975-2002 CIVIL WAR

1991 Dos Santos and Unita leader Jonas Savimbi sign peace deal on transition to a multiparty political system.

1992 Dos Santo wins presidential elections. Savimbi rejects results and resumes guerrilla war.

2002 Savimbi is killed and his guerrilla army transformed into a political party.

2011 Urban youth networks protest about government's failure to redistribute oil money.

2016 Low-scale armed separatist rebellion flare up again in Cabinda province.

2017 Inauguration of President João Lourenço.

ZIMBABWE p. 57-76

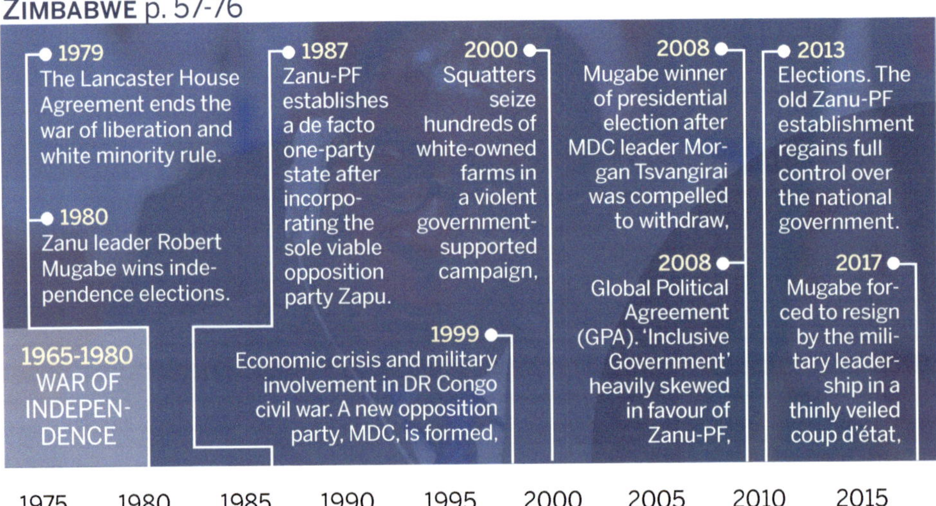

4. Southern African hot spots and hotbeds of conflict

Mozambique's RENAMO rebellion, uneven development and financial woes

Alongside Angola and the DRC, Mozambique is one of the SADC countries that have continued to experience armed conflict. After the 1992 General Peace Accord ended the civil war that started shortly after the country gained its independence, Mozambique was characterised by remarkable political stability and economic growth, and was, thus, often portrayed as Southern Africa's showpiece post-conflict state.[119] From 2012, however, the country saw an escalation of conflict, as the FRELIMO government's historic civil war adversary RENAMO (still led by the veteran Afonso Dhlakama) took up arms again, even as it continued to engage in parliamentary politics.[120] In 2016, moreover, Mozambique was plunged into a severe fiscal crisis, when it fell out with international financial institutions over secret loans to the FRELIMO government worth $2.2 billion.[121]

The renewed RENAMO insurgency and peace process

After Mozambique's independence in 1975, the FRELIMO government – which adopted a Marxist-Leninist doctrine and sought military support from the Soviet Union and East Germany – imposed sanctions on Rhodesia's white minority regime and harboured ZANU guerrillas, so that they could launch attacks across the border. The Rhodesian Front (RF) regime and its Central Intelligence Organisation (CIO) responded by clandestinely arming a Mozambican rebel army, RENAMO, to destabilise the FRELIMO government.[122] Shortly before Zimbabwe's independence, RENAMO was handed over to the South African apartheid regime's Directorate of Special Tasks, which sought to force the Mozambican government to abandon its support for the ANC by escalating a civil war and airlifting vast quantities of weaponry and supplies to support RENAMO.

---

119 Darch, Colin, 'Separatist tensions and violence in the "model post-conflict state": Mozambique since the 1990s', Review of African Political Economy, 43, 148 (2016), p. 320; Perez Nino and Le Billon, 'Foreign aid', p. 80.

120 Wiegink, Nikkie, '"It will be our time to eat": Former Renamo combatants and big-man dynamics in central Mozambique', Journal of Southern African Studies, 41, 4 (2015), p. 2.

121 Hanlon, Joseph, 'Following the donor-designed path to Mozambique's US$2.2 billion secret debt deal', Third World Quarterly, 38, 3 (2017), p. 753.

122 Chung, Re-Living the Second Chimurenga, p. 79; Stedman, Stephen John, Peacemaking in Civil War: International mediation in Zimbabwe, 1974–1980 (Boulder, Lynne Rienner, 1991); Vines, 'Renamo's rise and decline', p. 376.

From 1980, RENAMO was led by Dhlakama and by 1982 it numbered some 8,000 fighters. The movement became infamous for war crimes, such as the mutilation of civilians. By 1984, the guerrilla war had compelled the FRELIMO government to sign the Nkomati Accord with South Africa, whose regime subsequently reduced its covert support, while ensuring that RENAMO became more self-reliant. Military intervention by Tanzania and Zimbabwe – whose supply line to the harbour of Beira was disrupted by the war, the death of Mozambican President Samora Machel in a suspicious plane crash, and the introduction of reforms by his successor Joaquim Chissano in the era of perestroika – finally led to peace talks with RENAMO in 1990. Though an initial ceasefire collapsed, a General Peace Accord ending the civil war was signed in October 1992, at a time when drought and starvation had rendered RENAMO's guerrilla tactics unsustainable. The Accord envisaged a comprehensive DDR programme and a transition period leading to democratic elections overseen by UN peacekeepers.[123]

DDR saw substantial delays and several mutinies, and it proved impossible to reach the target of creating a 30,000-strong national army with equal numbers of fighters from the two civil war parties before the elections due to be held in 1994. Yet the newly created Mozambique Defence Armed Forces (FADM) became a pillar of stability. Although many RENAMO fighters lacked the basic qualifications for integration into the army, FADM was joined by numerous fighters who took the opportunity to earn a regular wage, as well as RENAMO cadres who continued to hold high-ranking positions in the army for decades to come.[124]

With the support of international donors, RENAMO transformed itself into a political party that, despite its war-time atrocities, succeeded in attracting a considerable support base and civilian cadres seeking an alternative to FRELIMO. Consequently, by 1995, former guerrilla fighters made up only a fraction of RENAMO's representatives in the national assembly. Attracting support mostly from Mozambique's central regions – an indication of the importance of ethnic politics – RENAMO gained nearly 40% of the vote in the 1994 and 1999 elections, but steadily lost electoral support thereafter. To some extent its electoral demise related to FRELIMO's economic success and its tactics of curbing the political space for its competitors, as well as instances of voter fraud. The demise was, however, also down to RENAMO's poor organisational capacity and lack of qualified cadres, the centralised (and poor) governance of the party by Dhlakama, a lack of leadership renewal, factionalism, and the misappropriation of state funds by RENAMO representatives at the expense of their constituents.[125]

In 2008, RENAMO's support base was undermined by the breakaway *Movimento Democrático de Moçambique* (MDM), which was partially banned from contesting the 2009 elections, but which went on to secure the position of mayor in Quelimane in

123 Chan, Stephen, Robert Mugabe: A Life of Power and Violence (London, I.B. Tauris, 2003), p. 33; Nuvunga, Adriano N. and Eduardo, Sitoe, 'Party institutionalisation in Mozambique: "The party of the state" vs the opposition', Journal of African Elections, 12, 1 (2012), p. 118; Vines, 'Renamo's rise and decline', p. 376.

124 Vines, 'Renamo's rise and decline', pp. 382–87.

125 Darch, 'Separatist tensions', p. 322; Vines, 'Renamo's rise and decline', pp. 382–87.

2011 and to win 17 constituencies in the 2014 parliamentary elections.[126] With RENAMO's fortunes waning (as the party proved unable to deliver services, to put forward a credible political programme or to field electable candidates), in 2009 Dhlakama relocated from the capital to the town of Nampula in northern Mozambique. Although effectively isolating himself, Dhlakama argued that this would allow him to reconnect to the electorate and prepare the resistance against the Marxist FRELIMO government, which (he alleged) held onto power by fraudulent means, whereas he had brought democracy to Mozambique.[127]

RENAMO leaders raised several grievances as the conflict escalated and turned violent. Veterans of the former guerrilla army felt disadvantaged vis-à-vis their FRELIMO counterparts in accessing pensions. This added to a general feeling of frustration and marginalisation among demobilised fighters in rural RENAMO strongholds.[128] RENAMO also further demanded that ex-combatants and officers should be integrated into the national army and its senior command structures, even though many of the veterans lacked the necessary skills to serve in the military.[129] Moreover, RENAMO denounced what it deemed FRELIMO's monopolisation of the state and access to its resources. Indeed, in the four decades that FRELIMO has been in office, the lines between party and state structures have, to some extent, become blurred: party-aligned officials have been deployed across state and parastatal institutions, a common phenomenon in dominant party systems. Politically connected individuals and FRELIMO veterans have benefited disproportionately from government contracts and large-scale foreign investments, as the FRELIMO government acts as a gatekeeper, privileging its peers and enabling them to accumulate wealth.[130] RENAMO also complained that FRELIMO members were the sole beneficiaries of Mozambique's newly discovered natural wealth – clearly, it too wanted a slice of the cake.[131] Moreover, as the conflict went on, RENAMO demanded greater devolution of power and the introduction of additional provincial administrations.[132]

The grievances highlighted by RENAMO – grievances that relate to the incomplete implementation of the General Peace Accord and its DDR programme, the authoritarian and nepotistic tendencies of the FRELIMO government, and the destitution of ex-combatants – nurtured a renewed outbreak of violence.[133] According to Macamo, however, the ambitions of the political entrepreneur, Dhlakama, who resorted to violence when his fortunes in parliamentary politics waned, constituted a principal

126 Vines et al., Mozambique to 2018, p. 19; Wiegink, '"It will be our time to eat"', p. 2.

127 Vines, 'Renamo's rise and decline', p. 386.

128 Vines et al., Mozambique to 2018, p. 27.

129 Elísio Macamo, interview, Basel, 22.11.17; Wiegink, '"It will be our time to eat"', p. 1.

130 Ganho, Ana, 'The murder of Gilles Cistac: Mozambique's future at a crossroads', Review of African Political Economy, 43, 147 (2016), p. 143; Elísio Macamo, interview, Basel, 22.11.17; Nuvunga and Sitoe, 'Party institutionalisation in Mozambique', p. 119.

131 Elísio Macamo, interview, Basel, 22.11.17; Vines, 'Renamo's rise and decline', p. 387.

132 Vines et al., Mozambique to 2018, p. 27.

133 Macamo, Elísio, 'Power, conflict, and citizenship: Mozambique's contemporary struggles', Citizenship Studies, 21, 2 (2017), p.196; Wiegink, '"It will be our time to eat"', p. 17.

driver of the conflict, and the escalation was facilitated by the fragile state's inability to prevent such criminal enterprises.[134]

From 2012 onwards, the FRELIMO–RENAMO conflict was characterised by sporadic violent clashes, raids by RENAMO and simultaneous talks. In late 2011, Dhlakama met President Armando Guebuza for the first time since the latter came to office six years earlier; but in March 2012, an armed confrontation between 300 RENAMO veterans, Dhlakama's 'Presidential Guard' and the riot police resulted in two fatalities. A further meeting between the leaders seemed to defuse the situation somewhat, but shortly thereafter Dhlakama threatened to train RENAMO supporters for combat and to split the country. The conflict escalated further in April 2013, when nine people were killed at Múxunguè in a clash between RENAMO supporters and police, who claimed that RENAMO was seeking to establish a military base. In an act of retaliation (which Dhlakama claimed to have ordered, although he subsequently retracted the statement), RENAMO attacked a local police station, leaving four police officers and an attacker dead. Over the subsequent months, clashes in central Mozambique continued with increasing frequency and intensity. Gunmen, for instance, killed five soldiers while raiding a military arms depot in June 2013; and rebels repeatedly ambushed motorists on Mozambique's main highway. The army, meanwhile, raided RENAMO camps, while RENAMO announced the creation of a rebel-held security perimeter as protection against government attacks. These clashes caused serious disruptions of mining activities, transport routes and tourism.[135] The violence continued in 2014 as RENAMO attacked cargo trains and civilians travelling along the main north–south route, and sought to expand its operations into further provinces. In mid-May, the army clashed with RENAMO rebels in Zambézia province.[136]

Although RENAMO could access the arms caches it had withheld during the DDR exercise after the civil war, and although it demonstrated its ability to unleash violence and wreak large-scale destruction, the ragtag militia (numbering an estimated 800–1,000 fighters) did not have the capacity to reignite a full-on civil war.[137] According to Vines, violence was RENAMO's sole leverage, helping Dhlakama (who sought to prevent himself and his movement from becoming irrelevant) to force the government into negotiations and concessions.[138] Macamo, however, questions whether Dhlakama pursued any coherent long-term strategy, suggesting that he was driven by short-term considerations and opportunistically responded to events without a consistent plan or clear positions.[139]

The armed insurgency coincided with the 2013 municipal elections, which RENAMO boycotted, and the 2014 general elections (ahead of which RENAMO declared a ceasefire to enable voters to register for the poll). The electoral playing field in the 2014 elections was skewed by the state media's extensive positive coverage of FRELIMO's

134 Elísio Macamo, interview, Basel, 22.11.17.
135 Vines, 'Renamo's rise and decline', pp. 386–88.
136 Vines et al., Mozambique to 2018, p. 23.
137 Wiegink, '"It will be our time to eat"', p. 1; Vines, 'Renamo's rise and decline', p. 388.
138 Vines, 'Renamo's rise and decline', p. 388.
139 Elísio Macamo, interview, Basel, 22.11.17.

well-resourced campaign, and was characterised by distrust, procedural irregularities, a partisan police force and a voter turnout of just 49%. While these irregularities were not sufficient to tip the scales at the national level, RENAMO nevertheless rejected the results, as it had done in every election since 1994. In fact, the party and its leader fared surprisingly well, gaining considerable ground compared to previous elections. In the parliamentary election, RENAMO won 89 seats, against FRELIMO's 144 and the MDM's 17, though it did not win an outright majority in any province. In the presidential election, Dhlakama came second with 36.6% of the vote, behind FRELIMO's Filipe Nyusi, who gained 57%, but ahead of the MDM's Daviz Simango (6.4%).[140]

RENAMO's surprisingly strong showing strengthened its bargaining position. Dhlakama instructed elected parliamentarians not to take up their seats. He threatened to proclaim an autonomous republic in northern and central Mozambique, and demanded the right to appoint the governors in those provinces where he had won a majority in the presidential race, or else RENAMO would continue to boycott parliament. The newly elected president, Filipe Nyusi, persuaded Dhlakama to take up RENAMO's parliamentary seats and introduced a bill formalising his demands; this, however, was rejected by the FRELIMO majority. This was followed by renewed calls for cessation, violent hostilities and a continued crisis that, ultimately, needed to be resolved at the negotiating table.[141]

Negotiations between the FRELIMO government and RENAMO had continued even as the violence unfolded: over a hundred rounds of talks took place between March 2013 and May 2015. The 2014 elections could be held thanks to a ceasefire and a fragile peace agreement, which contained amnesties for those responsible for the violence, and was signed by Dhlakama after parliament had approved changes to the electoral framework.[142] But the arrival in power of President Nyusi marked a turning point in the talks: his government appeared more willing to make concessions to RENAMO than had the administration of his predecessor, Guebuza.[143] Dhlakama's demand for special status for the candidate who came second in the election was eventually approved by the FRELIMO-dominated parliament. RENAMO's demands and the agenda for the talks included, among other issues, the integration of RENAMO cadres into the army, including a RENAMO demand that it should nominate the chief of staff. The politicisation of state institutions and party-state relations constituted a further talking point. RENAMO's demand for the devolution of power and the creation of autonomous provinces constituted a critical issue that resonated far beyond its support base, given the long-standing centralisation of power by the FRELIMO government and the widely perceived need for greater devolution of power.[144]

140 Vines et al., Mozambique to 2018, p. 19.

141 Macamo, 'Power, conflict, and citizenship', pp. 196–203.

142 Vines et al., Mozambique to 2018, p. 26.

143 Elísio Macamo, interview, Basel, 22.11.17.

144 Holanda Maschietto, Roberta, 'Decentralisation and local governance in Mozambique: The challenges of promoting bottom-up dynamics from the top down', Conflict, Security & Development, 16, 2 (2016), pp. 110; Ganho, 'The murder of Gilles Cistac', p. 142; Darch, 'Separatist tensions', p. 325.

Although negotiations over these issues faltered, a truce was reached, and in the course of 2016 and 2017 violent hostilities came to a halt. A not inconsequential part in this was played by the government's concession of a security perimeter for RENAMO rebels, from which the national army would stay away.[145] In order to stop the violence and RENAMO's raids, the state was thus compelled to relinquish control over parts of its territory and its internal sovereignty. The death of Dhlakama in May 2018 has raised hopes that in the absence of the ambitious veteran RENAMO leader an end to the conflict may become possible.[146] But the peace will remain fragile until such time as the grievances over centralised, authoritarian governance and economic marginalisation are addressed and Renamo fighters are demobilised.

The high-level negotiations between the government and RENAMO took place virtually without any consultation or input by civil society or the broader public. In the early stages of the talks, however, Mozambican academics and clerics did act as mediators. The local mediators, who found limited acceptance by the conflict parties, were later on replaced by international mediators, including representatives of the Italian government, which had been instrumental in brokering the 1992 Rome Accord. Several other Western donor nations that could possibly offer a peace dividend sought to support the peace process.[147] SADC, on the other hand, had no apparent role in the peace negotiations, as the regional body – dominated as it is by former liberation-party governments that are hostile to RENAMO – would not have been an acceptable mediator. Neither was the conflict addressed in any official Summit and Organ document, for SADC apparently treated the crisis as a matter of national, rather than regional security.

While the RENAMO conflict could be contained, in October 2017, a surge in violent attacks by what appeared to be a group of Islamist militants on police officers and civilians in northern Mozambique's Cabo Delgado province, where a sizeable Muslim community lives, raised concern about the arrival of violent religious extremism in Southern Africa. Over the coming months, the supposed jihadists launched some 20 brutal attacks in which over 50 people were killed. It remained, however, unclear whether the violence was primarily religiously motivated or whether it was mostly driven by poverty and marginalisation, state repression, or a struggle over the spoils from the extraction of minerals in northern Mozambique.[148]

Resource rents, redistribution and debt crisis

The extraction of mineral resources (including coal), the discovery of vast offshore gas fields, and the sustained and rapid economic growth that Mozambique has ex-

145 Elísio Macamo, interview, Basel, 22.11.17.

146 Fabricius, Peter, 'Could Afonso Dhlakama's death bring permanent peace to Mozambique?, ISS Today, 11.5.18.

147 Elísio Macamo, interview, Basel, 22.11.17.

148 Fabricius, Peter, 'Mozambique's first Islamist attacks shock the region: A new armed group calling itself al-Shabaab is spreading fear in a usually jihad-free region', ISS Today, 27.10.17; Fabricius, Peter, 'Mozambique's apparent Islamist insurgency poses multiple threats', ISS Today, 20.11.18; Elísio Macamo, interview, Basel, 22.11.17.

perienced over several years present both opportunities for development and risks of conflict. Extractive activities have resulted in the destruction of livelihoods and the resettlement of local communities, which, in some instances, were relocated to unsuitable land and were inadequately compensated. While the prospect of resource rents has heightened expectations of shared economic gain, the country lacks institutions that are strong enough to ensure that revenues are steered towards development and distributed transparently. In order to attract international investment, concessions to mine Mozambique's mineral wealth were granted on highly unfavourable conditions that generate little revenue for the state; this leaves Mozambicans, who depend on the state's investment in the country's human capital, feeling short-changed. The high levels of inequality and poverty render Mozambique vulnerable to conflict and in the foreseeable future may provoke further social unrest, similar to the riots that Maputo experienced in 2010.[149]

In 2016, Mozambique's economic growth prospects and stability were rocked by the revelation that the Guebuza administration had guaranteed $2,228 billion without informing parliament, the International Monetary Fund (IMF), donors or bondholders. The loans, which were set up in 2013, were used to purchase a tuna-fishing fleet and to establish several companies that were owned by the national intelligence agency to provide security for offshore gas and oil operations. The secret loans were provided by Credit Suisse and Russia's VTB Capital. Moreover, it was revealed that an additional $221 million in secret loans from other lenders had been directed towards the Ministry of the Interior between 2009 and 2014. In response to this disclosure, the IMF stopped the disbursement of a Standby Credit Facility loan in April 2016, and donors blocked their budget support to the Mozambican government.[150] The scandal and the freezing of donor assistance prompted an economic crisis and resulted in the adoption of a stringent austerity package that includes spending cuts in sectors that are essential to development and human security, including basic education and health.[151]

Angola's Cabinda conflict, youth protests, violent kleptocracy and transition of power

Peace took root in Angola after the leader of the *União Nacional para a Independência Total de Angola* (UNITA), Jonas Savimbi, was killed in 2002 and his guerrilla army

149 Hofmann, Katharina, 'Mozambique's economic transformation and its implications for human security', in A. Van Nieuwkerk and K. Hofmann (eds), Southern African Security Review 2013 (Maputo, Friedrich Ebert Stiftung, 2013), pp. 102, 116; Elísio Macamo, interview, Basel, 22.11.17; Nogueira, Isabela, Ollinaho, Ossi, Pinto, Eduardo Costa, Baruco, Grasiela, Saludjian, Alexis, Pinto, José Paulo Guedes, Balanco, Paulo and Schonerwald, Carlos, 'Mozambican economic porosity and the role of Brazilian capital: A political economy analysis', Review of African Political Economy, 44, 151 (2017), p. 114.

150 Hanlon, 'Following the donor-designed path', p. 765.

151 The Guardian, 'Mozambique fell prey to the promise of fabulous wealth – now it can't pay nurses', 27.1.17.

transformed into a political party. The MPLA government's military victory over UNITA ultimately put an end to more than four decades of war – the war of independence (1961-1974) and the civil war (1975-2001, with interludes).[152] Fourteen years on from Savimbi's death, Angola nevertheless continued to experience episodes of extreme violence, and a low-scale armed separatist rebellion flared up again in Cabinda province in 2016.[153] The formation of urban youth networks in 2011 to protest about the government's failure to redistribute the dividends of Angola's oil wealth, the lack of accountability by state officials, security forces that were responsible for boundless self-enrichment and human rights crimes, and unresolved questions of land rights and rural poverty – all these had considerable potential for violent conflict. The inauguration in 2017 of President João Lourenço, who succeeded Eduardo Dos Santos after the latter had been at the helm of the state and the MPLA for 38 years, marked a difficult transition of power, but raised hopes that Lourenço would end the grip of the Dos Santos clan, which had siphoned off billions of dollars from the state.[154]

The separatist struggle in Cabinda

Angola's northern Cabinda enclave, which has been the centre of the country's oil production since the 1960s (and by 1975 already produced 40% of the state's public revenue), has been the site of a separatist struggle for more than five decades. A separatist movement was formed as early as 1960, the year after oil was first discovered in the province, and became known as the *Frente para a Libertação do Enclave de Cabinda* (FLEC). Unlike the MPLA, which took control of Cabinda at independence, FLEC was not involved in any major military operations against the Portuguese colonial regime and experienced several splits in its early years.[155] While the South African and Western-sponsored UNITA guerrilla army financed its war efforts through the illicit mining of alluvial diamonds, in the 27 years of civil war it was the offshore installations in Cabinda, which were spared from the war and operated by Western petroleum companies, that provided the bulk of the socialist MPLA government's revenues. FLEC factions meanwhile sought to draw attention to their cause by staging low-level guerrilla attacks on Angolan government troops and by kidnapping foreign workers for ransom. After the civil war ended, the government cracked down on the Cabinda separatists, prompting a FLEC faction to sign a Memorandum of Understanding for Peace and Reconciliation in 2006. The frequency of hostilities was henceforth marked-

---

152 Birmingham, 'Angola', pp. 137–84; Ingles, 'The MPLA government', pp. 41–45.

153 International Crisis Group (ICG), Crisis Watch Database: Angola, 30.9.17, www.crisisgroup.org/crisiswatch/database

154 Didier Péclard, interview via email, 8.12.17 ; Roque, Paula Cristina, Reform or Unravel?: Prospects for Angola's transition (Pretoria, ISS, 2017), p. 5.

155 Le Billon, Philippe, 'Oil and armed conflicts in Africa', African Geographical Review, 29, 1 (2010), p. 71; Guimarães, Fernando Andresen, The Origins of the Angolan Civil War: Foreign intervention and domestic conflict (London and New York, Macmillan/St Martin's Press, 1998), p. 102.

ly reduced; but human rights abuses by the belligerents continued nonetheless.[156]

The conflict gained international attention when FLEC attacked the bus of the Togolese national football team, killing three and wounding eight, as it was being escorted by the Angolan military to a game in Cabinda during the 2010 African Cup of Nations.[157] The government stepped up its military presence and hold on the enclave, whose developmental backlog contrasts with its oil riches, arresting both alleged separatists and civil society activists. Government officials were moreover believed to be engaged in secret talks with FLEC.[158]

Violence flared again in March 2016, when FLEC militants claimed to have killed up to 30 government soldiers in several attacks.[159] Three months later, FLEC militants were reported to have boarded an offshore gas platform operated by Chevron, where they threatened foreign petroleum workers.[160] In February 2017, clashes between FLEC rebels and government troops left several people dead, with the army confirming two casualties.[161] While FLEC was able to launch such isolated attacks, it lacked the military capacity to become a threat to national stability. Moreover, it was hamstrung by deep factional divisions that were exacerbated by the death of its leader in exile in 2016.[162]

According to Péclard, in the past two decades, the MPLA government's response to the Cabinda rebellion has involved a multi-pronged approach. First, the government weakened FLEC by promoting the creation of a surrogate party, FLEC-Renovada. Secondly, the state clamped down hard on all civilian supporters of the Cabindan cause, including those demanding that the province should receive greater investment in health, education and social services in return for its oil riches, rather than outright secession. As part of this strategy, outspoken journalists and activists were jailed, while critical religious leaders were sidelined. Thirdly, rather than waging a sustained military campaign to root out FLEC, the Angolan army responded with limited but decisive strikes against the militants. This might be because the threat posed by FLEC provided the Dos Santos administration with a reason to maintain its security grip on Cabinda and, by extension, the entire country. While the Lourenço government may adopt a different approach, the armed separatist struggle in Cabinda may have been sustained because the manageable small-scale rebellion served the MPLA government's interests.[163]

---

156 Hodges, Tony, Angola: From Afro-Stalinism to petro-diamond capitalism (Oxford and Bloomington, James Currey/Indiana University Press, 2001), pp. 147–54; Le Billon, 'Oil and armed conflicts in Africa', p. 71.

157 The Guardian, 'Togo footballers were attacked by mistake, Angolan rebels say', 11.01.10.

158 Mail & Guardian, 'Oil-rich Cabinda the poorer for it', 28.9.12.

159 Mail & Guardian, 'Angolan rebels claim to have killed 30 troops; expecting "massive military invasion" from government', 24.3.16.

160 Reuters, 'Rebels alive and kicking in Angolan petro-province, oil workers say', 14.6.17.

161 Jeune Afrique, 'Angola: plusieurs morts dans des affrontements entre l'armée et les rebelles du Cabinda', 15.2.17.

162 Didier Péclard, interview via email, 8.12.17 ; Reuters, 'Rebels alive and kicking in Angolan petro-province, oil workers say', 14.6.17.

163 Didier Péclard, interview via email, 8.12.17.

FLEC indicated its readiness to engage in talks with the government.[164] But it is understood that the demand for autonomy – which enjoys neither significant national nor international support – would not be met, given that the offshore installations in Cabinda continue to produce the bulk of Angola's oil revenues.[165] While SADC's Double Troika expressed concern over the 2010 attack on the Togolese football team (which drew international attention to the region only months before South Africa hosted the 2010 World Cup), the Summit and Organ Troika remained silent on subsequent incidents, and generally took the line of the Angolan government on the Cabinda question.[166]

In April 2018, FLEC proposed a roadmap to peace and shortly after announced that it was seeking dialogue with the Angolan government to end hostilities. The peace efforts were, however, short lived: in February 2019, FLEC declared that it was resuming the armed struggle, claiming that the government had turned its back on the dialogue and was using violent repression. In the same month, the police reportedly arrested 77 separatist militants and sympathisers of the separatist movement. Meanwhile, a few months earlier the organisers of a public debate on Cabinda's autonomy had been charged with crimes against state security.[167] Nearly six decades after the outbreak of the secessionist rebellion, there was thus no peaceful solution to the Cabinda conflict in sight.

Rampant inequality, youth protests and state-sponsored violence

The advent of peace in Angola in 2002 was followed by a sustained period of formidable economic growth rates of some 15% per annum, fuelled by the country's oil riches, high commodity prices and economic diversification in the capital, Luanda, where urbanisation had already accelerated on account of the influx of people from rural areas into townships during the civil war.[168] By 2008, Angola's oil production had risen to 1.89 million barrels per day, and state spending on health was double the figure for 2002. However, the quality of health and education remained below the African average, and skyrocketing consumer prices put tremendous pressure on the livelihood of Angola's poor. Between 2000 and 2010, the cost of a basket of basic goods increased by 375%. By 2012, Luanda had become the most expensive city in the world (measured by the cost of living for expats), while 30.1% of Angolans lived on less than $1.90 a day in 2008.[169] Although, as part of the post-war reconstruction,

164 Cristina Udelsmann-Rodrigues, interview via email, 11.12.17.

165 Didier Péclard, interview via email, 8.12.17.

166 SADC, Double Troika Communiqué, Maputo, 14.1.10.

167 International Crisis Group (ICG), Crisis Watch Database, 12.3.19, www.crisisgroup.org/crisiswatch/database

168 Didier Péclard, interview via email, 8.12.17; Viegas, Sílvia Leiria, 'Urbanisation and peri-urbanisation in Luanda: A geopolitical and socio-spatial perspective from the late colonial period to the present', Journal of Southern African Studies, 42, 4 (2016), p. 604.

169 Weimer, Markus, The Peace Dividend: Analysis of a decade of Angolan indicators, 2002–12 (London, Chatham House, 2012), pp. 2–18; World Bank, Angola poverty headcount ratio at $1.9 a day (2011 PPP) (% of population), https://data.worldbank.org/indicator/SI.POV.DDAY?locations=AO, 27.1.18.

the government invested in new development initiatives – including electrification, water, housing, railway and industrial projects – the formidable peace dividend was not evenly distributed. Inequality spiked as politically connected elites (and the Dos Santos family, in particular) were able to accumulate enormous wealth, thanks to their involvement in such enterprises as the parastatal petroleum company Sonangol, while vast numbers of both rural and urban dwellers continued to live in poverty.[170] In many rural areas, access to agricultural land remained a source of tension. While peasants lacked access to arable land, farm land that had been given to senior military officers to reward their war efforts was underutilised. For land conflicts to be averted, a land reform and a review of the land tenure system is necessary.[171]

It was against this background of growing inequality and flagrant accumulation of wealth by elites that civic youth activist networks emerged in the wake of the 2011 Arab Spring. These sought political change and the resignation of President Dos Santos.[172] The protests – ignited by a popular hip-hop artist – gained momentum after the police arrested the leaders, prompting even bigger crowds to assemble in Luanda. The initial demand for Dos Santos to relinquish power widened into protests over poverty, civil rights and corruption, and sporadic small-scale protests continued to flare up over subsequent years. The wave of protests was an indication that a younger generation, which had not lived through the civil war, no longer accepted the war-time logic that equated dissent with treason.[173] Although the youth protests by the self-declared 'revolutionaries' were of great symbolic importance (given the subjugation of civil society after independence), the protests were confined to the cities of Luanda and Benguela, and never attracted more than 2,000 people. There was also unrest among demobilised soldiers, teachers and residents' associations of poor neighbourhoods, but networks were not established across these sectors.[174] While civil society remains rather poorly organised, according to Udelsmann-Rodrigues, by 2017 a proliferation and consolidation of civil society organisations could be observed.[175]

During Dos Santos' presidency, the state invariably responded to civic protests and media criticism with repression and police violence. Youth activists and journalists investigating human rights abuses committed by army officials in relation to the mining of diamonds were incarcerated, following trials that revealed the ineptitude of the prosecution authorities and the arbitrariness of the courts' judgments.[176] The arbitrary

170 Business Day, 'Angola's Sonangol investigates misconduct by Isabel Dos Santos', 20.12.17; Ovadia, Jesse Salah, 'The dual nature of local content in Angola's oil and gas industry: Development vs elite accumulation', Journal of Contemporary African Studies, 30, 3 (2012), p. 414; Didier Péclard, interview via email, 8.12.17.

171 Didier Péclard, interview via email, 8.12.17.

172 Didier Péclard, interview via email, 8.12.17 ; Vines, Alex and Weimer, Markus, Angola: Assessing risks to stability (Washington, DC, CSIS, 2011), p. 11.

173 Pearce, Justin, 'Youthful dissent challenges Angola's old elite', Current History, 115, 781 (2016), pp. 175–80.

174 Didier Péclard, interview via email, 8.12.17.

175 Cristina Udelsmann-Rodrigues, interview via email, 11.12.17.

176 Pearce, 'Youthful dissent', pp. 175–80.

application of the law and the lack of accountability by the seemingly untouchable security officials were particularly disconcerting in view of the repeated instances of extreme violence committed by the security forces.[177] In 2015, grisly reports emerged of a massacre during a police clampdown on a gathering of about a thousand members of the 'Light of the World' Christian church in Huambo province, UNITA's historic heartland in the central highlands and home to the Ovimbundu ethnic group. According to the government's official account, nine police officers and 13 civilians were killed in the incident at Mount Sumi, and the sect was portrayed as a threat to national security. Reports by journalists and opposition parties suggested that perhaps several hundred sect members had been killed and buried in mass graves. UNITA alleged a massacre by the special police forces, with over a thousand victims. Even if the actual death toll was only a tenth of what UNITA claimed, the Mount Sumi incident would still be the most lethal case of political violence in Southern Africa in the past decade and a half.[178] According to Roque, a clampdown on youth activists in 2016 resulted in the execution of over a hundred youths in Luanda's Viana township in the course of a single year.[179]

The Dos Santos family-state enterprise and the transition of power

The system of governance that the MPLA government established under Dos Santos after the civil war, Roque argues, rested on four pillars: the presidency, which centralised power in parallel structures and weakened the MPLA; the inflow of oil revenues from Sonangol, which fuelled an extensive patronage system and the elite's accumulation of wealth; the manipulation of foreign relations and financial partners to sustain the state apparatus and jumpstart the economy; and the securitisation of society and the state. From 2017, this system became increasingly unsustainable, and Dos Santos's successor has to embark on extensive reforms to prevent the MPLA's hegemonic control over the state and economy from unravelling.[180]

When, in September 2017, João Lourenço took over from Eduardo Dos Santos as president – a position occupied by the latter since 1979 – he was widely expected to preserve the elite's interests and those of the Dos Santos family, by maintaining their patronage system and access to the resources of the state. Instead, Lourenço spoke out against the monopolisation of the state and economy by the ruling clan, and undertook a series of bold moves apparently aimed at the power structures of the Dos Santos family. In his inaugural address, he hit out at monopolies in telecommunication, cement and other industries by companies owned by his predecessor's billionaire daughter, Isabel Dos Santos. After taking office, Lourenço abolished the government communications department, through which money was channelled to the Dos San-

177 Didier Péclard, interview via email, 8.12.17.
178 Orre, Aslak, 'Covering up a massacre in Angola?', CHR Michelsen Institute, 19.5.15.
179 Roque, Reform or Unravel?, p. 5.
180 Roque, Reform or Unravel?, p. 2.

tos family thanks to lucrative government contracts. Barely a month into his term, he replaced the central bank governor in an apparent effort to halt the illicit flow of money overseas. To the post of secretary for oil, Lourenço appointed a former Sonangol executive who had been dismissed by Dos Santos's daughter.[181] Most importantly, in November 2017, Lourenço removed Isabel Dos Santos from her post as the CEO of Sonangol, to which her father had elevated her, in a move that was viewed critically within the middle and lower ranks of the MPLA.[182] In late 2017, Sonangol announced an investigation into the possible misappropriation of funds by Isabel Dos Santos.[183] In September 2018, José Dos Santos, the former manager of the sovereign wealth fund and son of the former president who had stepped down as the leader of the MPLA a few days earlier, was detained on suspicion of various economic crimes, including embezzlement and fraud.[184]

Whether Lourenço's reforms go beyond curtailing the accumulation project of the Dos Santos clan remains to be seen at the time of writing. As Roque highlighted even before Lourenço took office, the new president will still need to maintain the MPLA's patronage system and salaries of the security apparatus. This will be at the expense of the population left outside the pool of beneficiaries. The Lourenço administration may also be seeking to carry out the minimum of reform needed to ensure the MPLA's continued control of Angola's state apparatus.[185]

Zimbabwe's unresolved crisis of governance and thinly disguised military coup

After the war of liberation and white minority rule ended in 1980, and after a wave of state-sponsored mass violence in the first years of its independence, Zimbabwe experienced a period of calm and stability. At the turn of the millennium, however, it was plunged into a deepening political and economic crisis – one that remains unresolved, although a SADC-brokered interim power-sharing government did restore a level of stability.[186] After the interregnum ended and ZANU-PF won the 2013 elections, the economy returned to stasis, the opposition fragmented, and civil society appeared para-

181 Financial Times, 'Angola's new president defies critics to shake up dos Santos elite', 8.11.17.

182 Business Day, 'Africa's richest woman gets fired', 15.11.17; Roque, Reform or Unravel?, p. 3.

183 Business Day, 'Angola's Sonangol investigates misconduct by Isabel dos Santos', 20.12.17.

184 International Crisis Group (ICG), Crisis Watch Database, 12.3.19, www.crisisgroup.org/crisiswatch/database

185 Roque, Reform or Unravel?, p. 3.

186 Aeby, 'Zimbabwe's gruelling transition', p. 16; Muzondidya, James, 'From buoyancy to crisis, 1980–1997', in B. Raftopoulos and A. Mlambo (eds), Becoming Zimbabwe: A history from the pre-colonial period to 2008 (Harare and Johannesburg, Weaver/Jacana, 2009), pp. 167–80; Raftopoulos, Brian, 'The crisis in Zimbabwe, 1998–2008', in B. Raftopoulos and A. Mlambo (eds), Becoming Zimbabwe: A history from the pre-colonial period to 2008 (Harare and Johannesburg, Weaver/Jacana, 2009), pp. 211–31.

lysed, despite a short social media-driven upheaval in 2016.[187] ZANU-PF's failure to resolve the succession of veteran President Robert Mugabe and to establish civilian control over the security sector eventually resulted in a thinly veiled coup d'état, when the military leadership intervened in favour of its preferred successor, Emmerson Mnangagwa, and compelled Mugabe to resign.[188] Although expressing concern about the de facto coup (which was denied by the military), SADC has proved incapable of responding decisively to the crisis into which Zimbabwe has again been spiralling since 2013.[189]

Zimbabwe's long descent into crisis and the SADC-brokered Global Political Agreement

The military coup of November 2017, which ended President Mugabe's hold on the highest office that he had occupied for 37 years, thanks to the support of the same military leadership that deposed him, provided a further twist in the two-decade Zimbabwean crisis. Following the Lancaster House Agreement, which ended the war of liberation against the white minority regime with a negotiated settlement in 1979, Zimbabwe saw a decade of remarkable calm in relations between the ZANU-PF government and the white settler population. But the 1980s witnessed the killing of at least 10,000 civilians by government troops in a campaign against the Zimbabwe African People's Union (ZAPU), ZANU-PF's fellow liberationists and the sole viable opposition party in the post-independence period.[190] ZANU-PF established a de facto one-party state after incorporating ZAPU in 1987, whereby the political and military elite of the former liberation army in government enforced political conformity and established a tight hold on state institutions, whose structures became intertwined with those of the party.[191]

In the second half of the 1990s, opposition to the ZANU-PF government started to form within civil society. This centred around discontent with authoritarian rule, corruption and management of the economy, which was ailing due to a bodged structural adjustment plan, the exorbitant cost of Zimbabwe's involvement in the Second Congo War, and the unbudgeted payment of pensions to war veterans. In 1999, a new civic movement spearheaded by the National Constitutional Assembly and the Zimbabwe

---

187 Aeby, Michael and Gideon Chitanga, 'Transforming an agrarian state with hashtags? Urban civil society and the quest for state transformation in Zimbabwe (2013–17)', paper presented at the 7th European Conference on African Studies, University of Basel, 30.6.17, p. 1.

188 Sabelo Ndlovu-Gatsheni, interview via Skype, 2.12.17.

189 SADC, SADC Organ Troika plus Council Chairperson Ministerial Meeting discusses the Political Situation in Zimbabwe, Press Release, 16.11.17.

190 Muzondidya, 'From buoyancy to crisis', pp. 167–80; Catholic Commission for Justice and Peace in Zimbabwe, Breaking the Silence, Building True Peace: A report on the disturbances in Matabeleland & the Midlands 1980–88 (Harare, 1999), p. 47; Phimister, 'The makings and meanings', pp. 197–99, 208.

191 Mazarire, Gerald, 'ZANU-PF and the government of national unity', in B. Raftopoulos (ed.), The Hard Road to Reform (Harare, Weaver Press, 2013), p. 79; Sachikonye, Lloyd, Zimbabwe's Lost Decade: Politics, development and society (Harare, Weaver Press, 2012), pp. 26–28; Bourne, Richard, Catastrophe: What went wrong in Zimbabwe? (London and New York, Zed Books, 2011), p. 120.

Congress of Trade Unions culminated in the formation of a new opposition party, the Movement for Democratic Change (MDC). After winning a constitutional referendum, the MDC threatened to defeat the ruling party in the 2000 elections. To curry favour with the land-hungry peasantry, the ZANU-PF government enabled a radical land reform that aimed at the expropriation of white farmers and, after being initially spearheaded by war veterans and youth militias, was retrospectively legalised. The fast-track land-reform programme empowered some 186,000 rural households over the coming years,[192] but resulted in the collapse of the formal economy, which revolved around the commercial agricultural sector. Thereafter, Zimbabwe was plunged into a multifaceted crisis that was characterised by dubious elections, violent state repression, a breakdown in the rule of law, sharp economic decline, and a deterioration both in relations with the Western powers, which were calling for regime change, and in the solidarity of African nations with the embattled ZANU-PF regime.[193]

In response to a violent police crackdown on an opposition gathering, which was organised by church and civil society organisations, and widely published images of battered MDC leaders on their release from custody, in 2007 SADC mandated South African President Thabo Mbeki to broker an early election. Rather than bringing stability, the resultant 2008 elections escalated the crisis. After a peaceful first round, in which the opposition won a parliamentary majority, the military orchestrated a campaign of violence against suspected MDC supporters during the presidential run-off; this led to the killing of up to 200 people, the beating of at least 5,000 and the displacement of 36,000.[194] Consequently, neither SADC nor the AU was willing to recognise Mugabe's re-election in what became a grotesque one-horse race after the opposition candidate, Morgan Tsvangirai, was compelled to withdraw from the run-off.[195]

Instead of calling on the discredited Mugabe regime to relinquish power, the AU Assembly mandated Mbeki to resume his efforts. After protracted negotiations, ZANU-PF and the main MDC formations – one led by Tsvangirai (MDC-T) and the other a splinter group led by Arthur Mutambara and Welshman Ncube (MDC-N) – signed a Global Political Agreement (GPA) in September 2008. Central to the GPA was the establishment of a power-sharing government, pending elections that would only be held in July 2013. The GPA also contained provisions relating to peace-building, reconciliation, constitutional and legislative reform, economic reconstruction, and security sector transformation that were meant to be implemented in the interregnum.[196]

---

192 The number of beneficiaries is an estimate from 2013. Prosper Matondi, interview, 19.7.13.

193 Raftopoulos, Brian. 'The labour movement and the emergence of opposition politics in Zimbabwe', Labour, Capital and Society, 33 (2000), pp. 256–79.

194 Human Rights Watch, Perpetual Fear: Impunity and cycles of violence in Zimbabwe (New York, 2011), p. 4; Masunungure, 'A militarized election', pp. 81, 86, 93.

195 Aeby, 'Zimbabwe's gruelling transition', p. 46.

196 Global Political Agreement, Agreement between the Zimbabwe African National Union-Patriotic Front (ZANU-PF) and the two Movement for Democratic Change (MDC) Formations, on Resolving the Challenges Facing Zimbabwe, 15.9.08, Harare, http://archive.kubatana.net/docs/demgg/mdc_zpf_agreement_080915.pdf, 3.1.14.

The balance of power in the resulting 'Inclusive Government', which was forever at risk of collapse, was heavily skewed in favour of ZANU-PF. The level of cross-party cooperation in the power-sharing executive varied depending on the portfolio, and only a few GPA provisions were fully implemented. An economic emergency plan did manage to stabilise the economy at a low level, after it had shrunk by 50% in the space of 10 years. Social services improved markedly and the completion of the prolonged constitution-making process represented a considerable achievement. Other GPA reforms aimed at opening the democratic space, enhancing transparency, building peace and monitoring the transition were either ignored or only partially implemented.[197] As a result, the 2013 elections – which ZANU-PF won with a landslide – went ahead without the reforms that were necessary to ensure a free and fair vote; thus, yet again, the outcome was disputed.

Despite glaring irregularities in the elections, which SADC observers described as 'free and peaceful' (rather than free and *fair*), SADC endorsed the outcome, in recognition of the fact that there had been a general absence of physical violence. It also rehabilitated Mugabe by electing him deputy chair of SADC.[198] The AU followed suit, making Mugabe chair of the Assembly in 2015.[199] Overall, the GPA process thus went to great lengths to ease the polarisation between the political elites and to restore a level of stability in the medium term. However, the interregnum did not decisively advance democratisation or create an institutional base on which to stabilise Zimbabwe in the long run.[200]

Economic standstill and informalisation

The period following the 2013 elections, during which the old ZANU-PF establishment regained full control over the national government, as well as urban constituencies where the party had fared poorly since the MDC came into existence, saw a gradual erosion of the limited economic gains of the GPA period. While Zimbabwe's average GDP growth in the five-year period in which the transitional governance process took place amounted to 8.8% (peaking at 11.9% in 2011), the rate dropped markedly after the elections: 3.2% in 2014 and a mere 0.6% in 2016 (according to World Bank data).[201] The poor economic performance related in part to drought conditions, which affected crop and livestock production and which in 2016 resulted in 4.1 million people (42% of the rural population) being exposed to acute food insecurity.[202]

197 Aeby, 'Zimbabwe's gruelling transition', pp. 395–400; Kanyenze, Godfrey, Kondo, Timothy, Chitambara, Prosper and Martens, Jos, Beyond the Enclave: Towards a pro-poor and inclusive development strategy for Zimbabwe (Harare, Weaver Press/LEDRIZ, 2011), p. 52.

198 SADC Election Observer Mission, 'Preliminary Statement', Harare, 2.8.13, p. 17; Zimbabwe Election Support Network, Report on the 31 July 2013 Harmonised Elections (Harare, 2013), pp. 6–9.

199 Aeby, 'Stability and sovereignty', pp. 272–91; SADC, 33rd Summit Communiqué, Lilongwe, 18.7.13, Para. 21, 22, 36.

200 Aeby, 'Zimbabwe's gruelling transition', pp. 413–16.

201 World Bank, World Data Bank: World Development Indicators, 2016.

202 SADC, SADC Regional Vulnerability Assessment, p. 35.

Continued sanctions by the United States – which, unlike the EU, refused to lift the targeted sanctions against regime representatives during the GPA period – played a role in perpetuating Zimbabwe's international image as a pariah state and possibly deterred some international investors.[203] However, the economic slump mostly resulted from the poor investment climate and the uncertainty stemming from the ZANU-PF government's contradictory economic and fiscal policies, long track record of corruption and mismanagement of public funds, and the sustained succession struggle and political instability.[204]

While the need for affirmative action to address colonial inequities was widely acknowledged, the Indigenisation and Empowerment Act – passed by the ZANU-PF-dominated parliament in 2007 and enacted in 2010 against the will of the MDC component of the power-sharing government – was widely found to undermine economic recovery plans.[205] According to the Act, companies worth more than US $0.5 million that were less than 51% owned by 'indigenous Zimbabweans' needed to 'cede a controlling interest' to persons (and the descendants of persons) who were disadvantaged by unfair racial discrimination before independence.[206] Economic experts widely agree that the Act scared away foreign investors, inhibited Zimbabwe's re-engagement with international financial institutions, and choked economic recovery by creating uncertainty. The policy primarily benefited the elites, while its supposedly broad-based component failed to genuinely empower communities. It was found to be conceptually flawed, in that it sought to distribute wealth without generating any additional wealth. Finally, the indigenisation policy was widely seen as a means of patronage for ZANU-PF-affiliated business elites, and as a populist panacea that promised immediate economic benefits to garner electoral support, rather than as a genuine development strategy.[207] In practice, the indigenisation policy was not rigorously enforced, and only a handful of indigenisation deals were concluded with foreign corporations. Although the indigenisation rhetoric was toned down after the 2013 elections, the resultant barriers to investment and insecurity have continued to inhibit Zimbabwe's economic recovery.[208]

---

203 Aeby, 'Zimbabwe's gruelling transition', pp. 204–08; Kanyenze et al., Beyond the Enclave, p. 43; Simba Makoni, interview, 15.3.13; Raftopoulos, 'The crisis in Zimbabwe', pp. 219, 284; Sachikonye, Zimbabwe's Lost Decade, p. 99.

204 Munyaradzi Nyakudya, interview via email, 1.12.17; Webster Zambara, interview via email, 10.12.17.

205 Aeby, 'Zimbabwe's gruelling transition', p. 354; Webster Zambara, interview via email, 10.12.17.

206 Indigenisation and Economic Empowerment (General) Regulations, Gazetted 29.1.10, First Schedule, Form IDG 01.

207 Andreasson, Stefan, 'Confronting the settler legacy: Indigenisation and transformation in South Africa and Zimbabwe', Political Geography, 29, 8 (2010), p. 424; Godfrey Kanyenze, interview, 09.8.13; Magure, Booker, 'Foreign investment, black economic empowerment and militarised patronage politics in Zimbabwe', Journal of Contemporary African Studies, 30, 1 (2012), pp. 78, 80; Daniel Ndlela, interview, 30.10.13.

208 Mlambo, Alois S., 'From an industrial powerhouse to a nation of vendors: Over two decades of economic decline and deindustrialization in Zimbabwe 1990–2015', Journal of Developing Societies, 33, 1 (2017), p. 112; Godfrey Kanyenze, interview, 09.8.13; Webster Zambara, interview via email, 10.12.17.

The ZANU-PF government's economic five-year plan that was launched in 2013 – the Zimbabwe Agenda for Sustainable Socio-Economic Transformation (ZimAsset) – was widely criticised for setting ambitious targets without offering any viable strategies for reaching them; it failed to halt economic decline.[209] According to Mlambo, by 2015 the government's poor policy choices since the 1990s had undermined the pillars of Zimbabwe's economy – agriculture, mining and manufacturing – to such an extent that an estimated 90% of the Zimbabwean population was unemployed and forced to scrape a living in the informal sector.[210] The poor economy, in turn, starved the state of revenue, so that some 90% of the tax collected went on salaries for civil servants, rather than on development projects.[211] In the GPA period, sales of diamonds from the Marange fields (discovered in 2006) resulted in at least some limited revenue for the state, though vast sums were siphoned off by the security establishment; but by 2014, the alluvial diamond deposits were exhausted and the revenue stream had dried up.[212]

In a further highly controversial decision, in November 2016 the government introduced bond notes through the Reserve Bank of Zimbabwe. These were distributed in response to the severe liquidity crunch that stemmed from the 2009 replacement of the Zimbabwean dollar, which had been rendered obsolete by hyperinflation, with a multicurrency system, including the US dollar. Rather than being an effective remedy for the cash shortage, it was feared that the pseudo-currency would bring back hyperinflation; and it merely helped the government mop up foreign currency, so that it could finance its own expenditure with hard currency.[213] A few months earlier, the government had caused a public outcry and revolt by cross-border traders when it banned the import of second-hand clothes and a range of basic goods from South Africa, in an apparent attempt to protect domestic industries. This ban, which the government was obliged to reverse, deprived informal sector traders of their livelihood.[214]

Demobilised civil society organisations and social media-driven upheaval

By 2016, widespread frustration over economic depression, corruption and the complacency of a gerontocratic regime that deprived young Zimbabweans of viable life

209 Business Day, 'Mugabe unveils five-year plan to save Zimbabwe economy', 23.10.13; NewsDay, 'ZimAsset, a failed economic policy', 20.9.17; The Standard, 'ZimAsset targets elusive', 17.7.16.

210 Mlambo, 'From an industrial powerhouse', p. 99.

211 Webster Zambara, interview via email, 10.12.17.

212 Dawson, Martin and Kelsall, Tim, 'Anti-developmental patrimonialism in Zimbabwe', Journal of Contemporary African Studies, 30, 1 (2012), p. 59; Kriger, Norma, 'ZANU PF politics under Zimbabwe's "power-sharing" government', Journal of Contemporary African Studies, 30, 1 (2012), pp. 13–21; Zimbabwe Independent, 'Diamond firms in comeback talks', 15.12.17; Ziminsky, Paul, 'Marange may not be the world's largest diamond producer for much longer', London Mining Journal, May 2014.

213 Nyamunda, Tinashe, Zimbabwe Bond Notes and Their Possible Long-term Legacy (Harare, 2017).

214 The New Age, 'Zimbabwe lifts ban on imports', 21.5.17; Chronicle, 'Govt relaxes regulations on second hand clothes imports', 19.1.17.

prospects prompted new social media-driven opposition movements and a short-lived popular upheaval in urban centres. This came about after the gradual erosion of the social base by the poor economy, ZANU-PF's 2013 election victory and the changing priorities of the donor community had plunged both established civil society organisations (CSOs) and the parliamentary opposition into a structural crisis.[215]

The organisational capacity and momentum of the vibrant liberal democratic civil society movement, which had driven the constitution-making process and launched the MDC, had been on the decline since the late 1990s.[216] Yet civil society continued to play a major role in the political dynamics of the next decade, and those CSOs that coalesced in the Save Zimbabwe campaign were instrumental in drawing international attention to the crisis and prompting a diplomatic intervention by SADC in 2007.[217] In the GPA period, the civic movement was divided on whether to engage in the Constitution Parliamentary Committee (COPAC) and the flawed transitional mechanisms of the elite-negotiated pact, or to oppose the GPA process. Assisted by donor funds, CSOs that embraced the GPA managed to improve their organisational capacity, and the ZANU-PF regime scaled down the level of crude repression when it was (unprecedentedly) held to account by SADC. The newly gained political space was used by CSOs, which seized the opportunity to contribute to the reforms envisaged, monitor implementation of the political transition agreement and promote the democratic agenda both domestically and internationally. The same period, however, saw the relationship between the civic democratic movement and the MDC-T deteriorate due to civil society's exclusion from transition mechanisms, the party's poor performance in government and corrupt tendencies.[218]

The conditions for civil society activism deteriorated markedly after ZANU-PF's 2013 landslide victory. The erosion of the civic democratic movement's social base of urban professionals and workers continued as the economy regressed. The campaign mounted by the established CSOs for political freedom and democracy became alien to the majority of Zimbabweans, who struggled to make a living in the informal sector and prioritised bread-and-butter issues. Meanwhile, ZANU-PF-aligned groups, which had been rallying around the demand for distributive justice for more than two decades, succeeded in gathering support among informal sector workers.[219]

Donor fatigue and the resulting withdrawal of funds meant that CSOs were compelled to scale down their operations or close altogether. Having funded CSOs for some 20 years in the hope of promoting a democratic transition, international donors changed their strategy and sought to engage the ZANU-PF government, after it had won a comparatively peaceful election and the political opposition disintegrated.

---

215 Aeby and Chitanga, 'Transforming an agrarian state with hashtags?', p. 7; Dorman, Understanding Zimbabwe: From liberation to authoritarianism (London, Hurst & Company, 2016), p. 7.

216 Dorman, Understanding Zimbabwe, pp. 170–74; Sachikonye, Zimbabwe's Lost Decade, pp. 137–43.

217 Raftopoulos, 'The crisis in Zimbabwe', pp. 227–32.

218 Aeby, 'Making an impact from the margins?', pp. 710–25.

219 Thilani Mswelanto, interview, 23.5.17; Raftopolous, Brian, 'The persistent crisis of the Zimbabwean state', SPT Brief, Johannesburg, Solidarity Peace Trust, 6 September 2016.

The new approach was premised on the misguided assumption that ZANU-PF would prove capable of transforming itself and providing a level of stability. Western donor nations, in the context of continued austerity, also redirected assistance towards regions of greater geopolitical importance than Zimbabwe. In some instances, the withdrawal of donor support related to the misappropriation of funds by civil society activists.[220] The paucity of donor funds translated into increased competition among CSOs that offered rare formal employment opportunities, thus adversely affecting CSO coordination.[221] This was exacerbated by a crippling leadership struggle and allegations of mismanagement in the Crisis in Zimbabwe Coalition, a nationwide network that played a key role in coordinating smaller organisations.[222] Most importantly, the established CSOs and the new protest movements failed to coordinate their campaigns, and the civic democratic movement remained divided over the question of whether or not to coalesce opposition parties.[223]

CSOs were moreover crippled by the same tools of repression that the regime had been using since the outbreak of the crisis, which included harassment, detention, prosecution, the denial of police clearance, infiltration, surveillance, police violence, and the abduction and murder of activists by security operatives.[224] In response to the use of social media by activists, the government drafted a Cyber Crime Bill, and communication platforms were temporarily disrupted.[225] This was combined with the denigration of activists in the state-controlled media.[226]

Owing to these conditions, the democratic civil society movement was effectively demobilised, and a sense of resignation took hold.[227] To stay relevant and respond to the altered structure of urban society, several CSOs underwent a thematic shift from political to economic rights, and drew up programmes focusing on issues such as access

---

220 Mail & Guardian, 'Zimbabwe's embattled NGO sector feels pinch', 30.5.14; Promise Mkwananzi, interview, 19.5.17; Thilani Mswelanto, interview, 23.5.17; The Zimbabwean, 'CIDA leaving Zim', 29.10.13; Zimbabwe Independent, 'NGOs, MDC-T hard hit by funding cut', 18.10.13; Raftopoulous, Brian, 'The threat of "normalising" authoritarianism in Zimbabwe', SPT Brief, Johannesburg, Solidarity Peace Trust, 18 October 2013.

221 Lucy Masingi, interview, 16.6.17; Vivid Gwede, interview, 20.5.17.

222 Aeby, 'Making an impact from the margins?', pp. 710–25; Financial Gazette, 'Crisis in crisis coalition', 11.12.14; Thilani Mswelanto, interview, 23.5.17; The Zimbabwean, 'I won't be pushed says Lewanika', 28.1.15; Linda Masarira, interview, 18.5.17; Mangoma Wadzanai, interview, 23.5.17; Vivid Gwede, interview, 20.5.17.

223 Vivid Gwede, interview, 20.5.17; Promise Mkwananzi, interview, 19.5.17; Thilani Mswelanto, interview, 23.5.17.

224 Promise Mkwananzi, interview, 19.5.17; Mangoma Wadzanai, interview, 23.5.17; Vivid Gwede, interview, 20.5.17; Linda Masarira, interview, 18.5.17; Mail & Guardian, 'Kidnapping rattles Zim activists', 13.3.15; The Star, 'Zim army warns cyber protesters: Head declares war on activists using social media "as weapon"', 6.8.16; The Zimbabwean, 'Suspected security operatives scare YAT', 25.7.13.

225 The Star, 'The unassuming hero of a revolution', 9.7.16; Herald, 'Cyber Crime Bill: The details', 17.8.16.

226 Vivid Gwede, interview, 20.5.17; Herald, 'Manipulation – Bane of the west', 17.12.13; Herald, 'Where are the NGOs?', 17.10.13; Herald, 'Time for patriotic think-tanks', 6.11.13.

227 Lucy Masingi, interview, 16.6.17; Promise Mkwananzi, interview, 19.5.17.

to education, basic services, housing and sustainable livelihoods.[228] Moreover, new organisations focusing on the rights and empowerment of vendors gained prominence.[229] The issues of economic rights had, however, long since been occupied by ZANU-PF and its affiliates.[230]

The socio-economic grievances and structural crisis of civil society organisations provided the background for the emergence of a new wave of loosely structured protest movements. The first to gain prominence was Occupy Africa Unity Square, whose leader, Itai Dzamara, together with a small group of brave demonstrators, staged protests outside parliament in October 2014, thereby gathering a large Facebook following.[231] Police violence and the disappearance of Dzamara – assumed to have been abducted and murdered by security operatives in March 2015 – sparked an outcry among human rights groups, the diplomatic community and the independent press that contributed to the emergence of further movements.[232]

The social media-driven protest movement that gained the most traction was #ThisFlag, which started on Independence Day in March 2016 with an emotive video posted by a young charismatic pastor, Evan Mawarire, which went viral. #ThisFlag's messaging appealed to the frustration and aspiration of young people: it spoke out against corruption, injustice and poverty, and sought to restore the dignity of those who had been deprived of personal opportunities by the crisis. Most brilliantly, #ThisFlag challenged ZANU-PF's efforts to monopolise the nationalist discursive repertoire by turning the national flag into a symbol of resistance, calling on people to wear the flag, and declaring love for the country that the movement wanted to reclaim. While taking up day-to-day grievances, Mawarire stayed clear of the language of liberal democracy that was associated with the worn-out MDC and NGOs, and sought instead to take a non-partisan stance. However, #ThisFlag's outspoken critique was directly aimed at ZANU-PF and corrupt officials.[233] In addition to several online and physical campaigns revolving around corruption and bond notes, #ThisFlag successfully drove the #ZimShutDown campaign, which in July 2016 effectively brought the country to a standstill.[234] Calls for further stayaways, however, gained little support and the move-

228 Vivid Gwede, interview, 20.5.17; Lucy Masingi, interview, 16.6.17; Thilani Mswelanto, interview, 23.5.17; Promise Mkwananzi, interview, 19.5.17; Linda Masarira, interview, 18.5.17; Vivid Gwede, interview, 20.5.17.

229 Mangoma Wadzanai, interview, 23.5.17.

230 Lucy Masingi, interview, 16.6.17; Raftopoulos, Brian, 'The 2013 Elections in Zimbabwe: The End of an Era', Journal of Southern African Studies, 39 (2013), pp. 981–84.

231 The Standard, 'Is Itai Dzamara the dreamer we lack?', 18.11.14; The Standard, 'Does Dzamara's approach work in Zim?', 23.11.14.

232 NewsDay, 'Police search for kidnapped journalist', 11.3.15; NewsDay, 'Civic society groups threaten more demos over Dzamara', 17.3.15; NewsDay, 'Local EU statement on the abduction of Itai Dzamara', 9.6.15; The Zimbabwean, 'Police savagely beat protester Itai Dzamara', 7.11.14; The Standard, 'Police crush Occupy Africa Unity protest', 12.6.16.

233 These observations are based on a review of the messages posted on the Facebook and Twitter accounts of Evan Mawarire between 1.2.16 and 30.2.17.

234 Financial Mail, 'When fear loses power', 14.7.16; Sunday Times, 'We are fed up and we are not afraid', 10.7.16.

ment ultimately lost momentum after Mawarire was charged with instigating public unrest and fled into exile in the United States.[235] Mawarire's success inspired similar movements, such as #ThisGown (which drew attention to the plight of unemployed graduates) and #Tajamuka (we are outraged). The latter was, however, run by seasoned activists with strong links to the MDC-T who sought to piggyback on the momentum created by #ThisFlag.[236]

The resounding (though short-lived) success of the new wave of protest movements could be explained by the void left by NGOs; the timing of their emergence, when public frustration with economic hardships had reached a new level; the availability of salient issues like bond notes and import bans; the vagueness of their messages; the use of relatively new social media; the multiplication effect of extensive mass media coverage; and the outstanding rhetorical skills of protest leaders such as Pastor Mawarire.[237] Yet, the protest movements were a flash in the pan, rather than a sustainable vehicle to decisively advance the transformation of the authoritarian state that lay at the heart of the crisis. The movements proved unsustainable, because they ran into the same limitations as the repressive state imposed on NGOs. More importantly, the movements were built around a few personalities, were poorly coordinated and lacked bureaucratic structures to sustain themselves and to develop policy alternatives that went beyond the ad hoc articulation of protest messages. Finally, although protest leaders claimed to make inroads into rural areas, the social media-driven movements were unlikely to gain significant support among the peasantry, which makes up the majority of Zimbabwe's population, and thus remained a largely urban and diaspora phenomenon.[238] A social media-driven revolution like the Arab Spring, which was carried out by the urban masses, was thus unlikely to succeed in the agrarian society of Zimbabwe.[239]

Fragmented opposition, coalition-building and electoral reform

After ZANU-PF's 2013 landslide victory, the parliamentary opposition consisting of the two MDC formations equally descended into crisis and disintegrated. Since its formation in 1999, the MDC had consisted of a broad spectrum of interest groups, ranging from trade union, student and human rights activists to business people and academics who coalesced owing to a common interest in deposing the authoritarian ZANU-PF regime and resolving the economic crisis. Notwithstanding considerable tensions between the party constituents over contradictory policy preferences, the breakaway of the small Matabeleland-based MDC-N from the MDC-T in 2005 was prompted by a leadership struggle between the MDC's secretary, Ncube, and its presi-

235 The Star, '#ThisFlag pastor arrested at Zim airport but still vlogging', 3.2.17.

236 Promise Mkwananzi, interview, 19.5.17; Thilani Mswelanto, interview, 23.5.17; The Star, 'Zimbabweans in anti-bond notes riot', 4.8.16; Mail & Guardian, 'Turbulent Zim faces a grim 2017', 15.12.16.

237 Aeby and Chitanga, 'Transforming an agrarian state with hashtags?', p. 7.

238 Lucy Masingi, interview, 16.6.17; IOL, 'Pastor spreads word of Zimbabwe's plight', 3.8.16.

239 Aeby and Chitanga, 'Transforming an agrarian state with hashtags?', p. 1.

dent, Tsvangirai, over the influence of unelected parallel structures, a lack of accountability and the decision to boycott senate elections.[240] In the power-sharing period, intraparty competition and hierarchies in the MDC-T that were upset by the elevation of cadres to government posts impeded the party's performance in the unity government and the coordination between the offices of Prime Minister Tsvangirai and Minister of Finance Tendai Biti. Infighting ahead of party-internal elections, moreover, absorbed a great deal of the human and financial resources of the (poorly resourced) party. The MDC-N's weight in parliament and the unity government was diminished by the continued fragmentation of the fringe party. MDC-N legislators defected and the deposed MDC-N president, Mutambara, refused to vacate his government office, becoming an instrument for Mugabe to divide the MDC formations.[241]

In the months following the 2013 elections, a rift between Tsvangirai, who clung to the party presidency, and a 'renewal team' led by Secretary General Biti and Elton Mangoma that sought to depose him widened rapidly. This was followed by months of public recriminations, intraparty violence, mutual suspensions from the party and court battles that by mid-2014 had resulted in yet another split.[242] Tsvangirai, as with MDC-N's breakaway nearly a decade earlier, continued to command the bulk of popular support and remained in control of the main faction. The renewal camp, meanwhile, sought to rope in other fringe parties, including the MDC-N.[243] The latter, however, equally continued to fragment, as prominent party leaders launched their own projects. None of these splinters, which revolved around a handful of personalities, succeeded in developing a viable party structure. Owing to these quarrels and the expulsion of leaders, the opposition's parliamentary representation vis-à-vis ZANU-PF was further diminished. Given the self-deprecation of the opposition and the continuous quarrels of its leaders, it came as little surprise when funders withdrew their support.[244]

The fragmentation was followed by renewed efforts to build a coalition among opposition parties, in the hope of standing a chance in the 2018 elections. Coalition talks took place between: the MDC-T and the breakaway formations; a ZAPU faction that had withdrawn from the historic Unity Accord with ZANU-PF in 2008; the Zimbabwe People First (ZimPF) and the National People's Party (NPP) that had been founded by former Deputy President Joice Mujuru following her expulsion from ZANU-PF

240 Raftopoulos, Brian, 'Reflections on Opposition Politics in Zimbabwe: The Politics of the Movement for Democratic Change', Reflections on Democratic Politics in Zimbabwe, Brian Raftopoulos and Karin Alexander (eds.), (Cape Town, Institute for Justice and Reconciliation, 2006), pp. 6–28.

241 Aeby, 'Zimbabwe's gruelling transition', p. 401.

242 Mail & Guardian, 'Endgame looms for Tsvangirai', 2.5.14; Mail & Guardian, 'Morgan Tsvangirai "suspended" by MDC', 27.4.14; NewsDay, 'Mangoma takes MDC-T to court', 23.3.14; NewsDay, 'MDC-T suspends Elton Mangoma', 19.2.14.

243 Mail & Guardian, 'Fast forward to a new Zimbabwe', 11.7.14; Mail & Guardian, 'Grand coalition imminent in Zimbabwe', 17.4.14; Mail & Guardian, 'Tsvangirai beats Biti in grassroots support', 09.5.14; Munyaradzi Nyakudya, interview via email, 1.12.17.

244 Sabelo Ndlovu-Gatsheni, interview via Skype, 2.12.17; Webster Zambara, interview via email, 10.12.17.

in 2015. That the former ZANU-PF representatives had been complicit in the regime's plunder of national resources and violent oppression apparently presented no obstacle to an electoral coalition for the MDC leaders.[245] Mujuru eventually launched the People's Rainbow Coalition, which came to include Dumiso Dabengwa's ZAPU.[246] In August 2017, Biti and Ncube joined the MDC Alliance led by Tsvangirai, in a move that alienated cadres from Matabeleland in the MDC-T and in Biti's People's Democratic Party, who opposed reunification with their local competitor.[247] The opposition was, however, set for further leadership struggles, as the MDC-T's long-term leader, Tsvangirai, underwent cancer treatment, and the alliance was headed by his lieutenants, who competed for the MDC-T leadership.[248] Tsvangirai – who had turned the co-opted labour movement into a formidable opposition force, brought together a broad coalition of societal forces in the MDC, sought to advance the democratic and economic reform agenda as prime minister during the gruelling power-sharing process, and remained by far the most popular opposition leader – succumbed to cancer in February 2018.[249]

The coalition-building efforts would reap little benefit if the electoral playing field, as in previous elections, remained skewed against the opposition. Notwithstanding sustained campaigns by the Zimbabwe National Electoral Reform Agenda and the Electoral Reforms Working Group (which consisted of opposition parties and CSOs, respectively), the major grievances of the electoral framework that emerged from the 2013 vote remained unresolved as Zimbabwe headed into the 2018 elections. The independence of the Zimbabwe Electoral Commission (ZEC), whose credibility had been compromised by irregularities in the management of the 2013 election, remained doubtful. Under the new constitution, the voters' roll was managed by the ZEC, rather than the blatantly partisan veteran registrar general. However, the shambolic and highly inaccurate electoral roll, which had undermined the transparency of the voting process in 2013, still needed to undergo a transparent audit. The voter registration process that had resulted in the disenfranchisement of thousands of suspected opposition supporters in urban constituencies in the previous election remained an area of concern. Most importantly, key state institutions, the security sector in particular, remained untransformed. This raised concerns about a potential state-sponsored campaign of electoral violence, as witnessed in the elections held between 2000 and 2008, or systemic intimidation, as in 2013.[250]

---

245 Chronicle, 'Mujuru forms new party', 4.3.17; Financial Gazette, 'Joice Mujuru's party splits', 9.2.17; Guardian, 'Joice Mujuru: The woman threatening to topple Robert Mugabe's ruling party', 28.7.15.

246 Munyaradzi Nyakudya, interview via email, 1.12.17; NewsDay, 'Mujuru, Biti, Dabengwa form own coalition', 23.9.17.

247 Sabelo Ndlovu-Gatsheni, interview via Skype, 2.12.17; Munyaradzi Nyakudya, interview via email, 1.12.17; Reuters, 'Zimbabwe opposition reunites to challenge Mugabe', 05.08.17.

248 NewsDay, 'MDC Alliance root for Chamisa', 15.1.18; NewsDay, 'MDC Alliance leaders in crisis meeting', 6.2.18.

249 The Guardian, 'Morgan Tsvangirai, Zimbabwe opposition leader, dies aged 65', 14.2.18.

250 Research & Advocacy Unit, Zimbabwe since the Elections in July 2013 (Harare, 2017), pp. 371–94.

ZANU-PF's succession struggle and the thinly disguised military coup

The greatest source of instability in the period after the 2013 elections remained the ZANU-PF regime, its military component and the ruling party's inability to renew its geriatric leadership. Factional struggles had been a constant feature of the party since Mugabe broke away from ZAPU in 1963 to found ZANU. While the party leadership violently quelled several rebellions and neutralised competitors during the war of liberation, the previous allegiance to ZANU or ZAPU became the major dividing line after ZANU-PF forcibly incorporated ZAPU through the Unity Accord. The modalities of the Accord, the divide between progressive and intransigent forces and competition along ethno-linguistic lines, together with the internal politics of provincial branches and the personal ambitions of senior leaders, provided the parameters for a sequence of succession struggles over Mugabe's place at the helm of the state and party.[251] Although the question of succession had been bubbling under the surface ever since Mugabe became executive president in 1987, a succession plan never materialised, as Mugabe muted the debate and skilfully played off the different camps in his party against each other in order to stay in power.[252]

The question of succession came to a head at ZANU-PF's 2004 Congress, when Joice Mujuru, a war veteran and Zezuru married to the wealthy and well-connected retired General Solomon Mujuru, became deputy president, rather than Emmerson Mnangagwa, a Karanga oligarch. It was believed at the time that Mujuru would succeed Mugabe after the next general election. A plot by Mnangagwa supporters to prevent Mujuru's election as vice president backfired and resulted in the expulsion and demotion of the conspirators, who were, however, gradually rehabilitated by Mugabe in the following years.[253] Since Mugabe hung onto power, a group of moderate reformers in the ZANU-PF politburo who feared that the party would lose the election if Mugabe ran for another term fielded Simba Makoni as an alternative ZANU-PF candidate for the 2008 elections. He, however, was expelled from the party.[254]

While former ZAPU stalwarts pulled out of the Unity Accord in the wake of the violent 2008 election crisis, the existential threat that the electoral defeat, international pressure and power-sharing talks posed for ZANU-PF prompted its cadres to close ranks. The covert race for Mugabe's succession nevertheless remained a burning issue throughout the GPA period, and took a dramatic turn when Solomon Mujuru was killed in a conflagration.[255] It was suspected that hardliners from the Mnangagwa camp

---

251 Aeby, 'Zimbabwe's gruelling transition', p. 65; Simba Makoni, interview, 15.3.13.

252 Mandaza, Ibbo. 'Will ZANU PF Survive After Mugabe?', In The Day After Mugabe, Gugulethu Moyo and Mark Ashurst (eds.), (London, Africa Research Institute, 2007), 39–45; Gerald Mazarire, interview, 25.10.13; Dumiso Dabengwa, interview, 30.6.13.

253 Mandaza, 'Will ZANU PF survive after Mugabe?,' p. 41; Mazarire, 'ZANU-PF and the government of national unity', p. 98.

254 Simba Makoni, interview, 15.3.13; Dumiso Dabengwa, interview, 30.6.13.

255 Aeby, 'Zimbabwe's gruelling transition', p. 67; Chan, Stephen, and Ranka Primorac. 'Postscript: Making Do in Hybrid House.' In Zimbabwe Since the Unity Government, Stephen Chan and Ranka Primorac (eds.), New York, Routledge, 2013, pp. 119–23. New York: Routledge, 2013, p 119. Ibbo Mandaza, interview, 6.11.13.

had killed the oligarch, with whom they were in competition over political power and control of the Chidazva diamond fields.[256] The depth of the factional divide also became apparent in tumultuous elections for ZANU-PF's grassroots District Coordination Committees and repeated appeals at party conferences to shun factionalism.[257] Yet, the succession issues were muted at party congresses, and the elective conferences held under the GPA endorsed the octogenarian both as presidential candidate and party leader. The factional fights in ZANU-PF, alongside those in the rival MDCs, affected the GPA process, as the accommodation of factions contributed to the appointment of a massively bloated executive. The inability to resolve the succession question resulted in the suspension of a contested running mate clause for presidential elections in the COPAC constitution, and hardliners from the Mnangagwa camp were blamed for sabotaging reforms, while Mujuru showed willingness to work with the MDC. Although the Mujuru faction was portrayed as the moderate wing, relative hardliners (with ties to the security sector establishment) and progressives could be found on both sides of the divide. Career prospects and patronage networks were at least as important for factional alignments as policy preferences.[258]

The succession struggle between Mujuru and Mnangagwa that lasted for a decade ended with Mujuru's removal from the office of vice president in late 2014, and the expulsion of her supporters from ZANU-PF. Among other allegations, Mujuru was accused of having plotted to unseat Mugabe and of having worked with Western intelligence services to undermine the Zimbabwean government. Mnangagwa, on the other hand, was appointed vice president, and thus became set to succeed Mugabe.[259] Mnangagwa's victory over Mujuru owed much to the backing of the army chief, Constantino Chiwenga, the use of the state intelligence organisation against his competitors, and the support of Mugabe, who eventually decided to take his side.[260]

Rather than ending the struggle to succeed Mugabe, Mujuru's expulsion marked the beginning of yet another contest for the party leadership that pitted Mnangagwa's camp of liberation-struggle stalwarts (which, in a reference to his nickname 'Crocodile', became known as 'Lacoste') against the 'Generation 40' (G40) that was headed by the first lady, Grace Mugabe, and comprised a group of younger ZANU-PF cadres. While Mnangagwa, who had been in government since independence, was said to have snubbed these aspiring personalities, who generally lacked struggle credentials, the infighting was driven by both ambition for power and tangible economic interests, as the competing elites' accumulation projects depended on continued access to political power.[261]

256 International Crisis Group, 'Resistance and denial: Zimbabwe's stalled reform agenda', Africa Briefing, 82 (16 November 2011), p. 15; Kriger, 'ZANU PF politics under Zimbabwe's "power-sharing" government,' p. 22; Mail & Guardian, 'Zim general's death', 29.3.12.

257 Herald, 'ZANU-PF DCC elections postponed', 10.1.12.

258 Aeby, 'Zimbabwe's gruelling transition', pp. 70, 402.

259 Herald, 'ZANU-PF expels Joice Mujuru', 3.4.15; Reuters, 'Zimbabwe's Mugabe names "The Crocodile" Mnangagwa as deputy', 10.12.14.

260 Sabelo Ndlovu-Gatsheni, interview via Skype, 2.12.17; Munyaradzi Nyakudya, interview via email, 1.12.17; Raftopoulos, Caught between the Croc and Gucci City.

261 Raftopoulos, Caught between the Croc and Gucci City; Webster Zambara, interview via email, 10.12.17.

Grace Mugabe, who was thought to have ambitions to become vice president and eventually to succeed her husband, became chair of the ZANU-PF Women's League, and the G40 was backed by the Youth League. By mid-2016, it became clear that the G40 equally enjoyed the support of President Mugabe – and in fact, appeared to have become his own project. Mnangagwa, meanwhile enjoyed the support of the Zimbabwe National Liberation War Veterans Association, which broke ranks with Mugabe for a second time in its post-independence history; however, he was unable to embrace this support fully, as it would have been presented as evidence of his disloyalty to Mugabe. By mid-2017, the scales had tipped against Lacoste, and Mnangagwa was publicly vilified in the state media, being accused of trying to unseat Mugabe.[262] In October 2017, Mugabe demoted or sacked Mnangagwa supporters in a surprise cabinet reshuffle, while allocating the most influential ministerial portfolios to G40 representatives.[263] Finally, on 7 November, he dismissed Mnangagwa as vice president on the grounds of alleged disloyalty.[264]

By dismissing Mnangagwa, who was the preferred successor of the military leadership that had kept Mugabe in power, the 93-year-old president had committed a severe strategic mistake. A few days later, General Chiwenga, in the presence of the senior commanders of the armed forces, made a public statement in which he demanded an immediate halt to the purges of liberation leaders (i.e. Mnangagwa supporters) from state and party structures. As in previous political statements by the military leadership, Chiwenga insinuated that the army, as the custodian of the legacy of the liberation struggle, would intervene if counter-revolutionary elements threatened to reverse the gains of the armed struggle. In contrast to previous political statements by the military, however, the coup threat was directed not against the opposition parties, but against ZANU-PF's G40.[265] At this point, the International Crisis Group suggests, Chiwenga was aware of a plan to purge him and other military officers, alongside Mnangagwa, who had fled to Mozambique in fear of his life.[266] Chiwenga's interference in civilian politics was denounced by a ZANU-PF spokesperson as the G40 leadership apparently underestimated the resolve of the military commanders.[267]

In the early hours of 15 November, Major General Sibusiso Moyo announced on national television that the military was stepping into the political fray to stabilise the deteriorating political, social and economic situation. The army was, therefore, conducting an operation against criminals around President Mugabe who were causing suffering in the country, in order to allow a return to normality. The camouflage-clad

262 Pigou, Piers, 'Standoff in Zimbabwe as Struggle to Succeed Mugabe Deepens', Johannesburg: International Crisis Group, November 14, 2017, p 1.

263 NewsDay, 'Mugabe in shock cabinet reshuffle', 10.10.17.

264 Southall, Roger, 'Bob's Out, the Croc Is In: Continuity or Change in Zimbabwe?', Africa Spectrum 17 (2017): 81–94.

265 Raftopoulos, Caught between the Croc and Gucci City.

266 International Crisis Group, 'Zimbabwe's "military-assisted transition" and prospects for recovery', Africa Briefing (20 December 2017), p. 4.

267 Raftopoulos, Caught between the Croc and Gucci City.

Major General, as well as military and political officials who explained the events in subsequent statements, were at pains to stress that the intervention was not a military takeover and that Mugabe was still president. This was because an undisguised coup would have been unacceptable to the African Union and SADC, and would have prompted international sanctions. While Mugabe and his family were held at his residence, G40 members were arrested. As the commissioner general of police was affiliated to G40, images of policemen who were held captive were circulated on social media as a demonstration of power.[268]

The military operation was a thinly disguised coup d'état to ensure that Mnangagwa succeeded Mugabe and to secure the supremacy of the liberation war generation. To maintain the legal veneer of the 'military-assisted transition of power', the securocrats were relying on the president agreeing to step down. The intransigent nonagenarian autocrat, however, clung onto power.[269] The coup leaders, Raftopoulos explains, therefore used a three-pronged strategy. First, they continued to refer to Mugabe as the president and commander-in-chief of the armed forces in all official communications. Secondly, war veterans staged a 'Mugabe must go' march that was joined by thousands, to display the support of the populace for the military's actions. Thirdly, on 19 November, the ZANU-PF central committee, while thanking the military for its intervention, expelled 20 members of the G40, removed Mugabe from the party presidency and recommended that he step down from the office of head of state. The central committee also reinstated Lacoste cadres, elected Mnangagwa as its interim president and nominated him to become head of state.[270]

Having been dismissed from the party, whose figurehead he had been since founding it in 1963, Mugabe addressed the nation in what was expected to be his resignation speech. In his bizarre address, the geriatric president acknowledged the perils facing national stability and affirmed the legality of the military intervention, but – assuming that he was still in charge – failed to announce his resignation.[271] Consequently, war veterans demonstrated against their former patron the next day, and Mnangagwa, who justified the military intervention (dubbed 'Operation Restore Legacy') as protecting the ethos of the liberation struggle against British colonialism, called on Mugabe to step aside. Meanwhile, a parliamentary motion for Mugabe to be impeached was tabled, co-sponsored by the MDC-T and ZANU-PF.[272] When parliament sat to debate the impeachment on 21 November, Mugabe finally tendered his resignation as president of the Republic of Zimbabwe in a letter that was read out by the speaker, Jacob Mudenda.[273]

---

268 International Crisis Group, 'Zimbabwe's "military-assisted transition" and prospects for recovery', p. 4; Raftopoulos, Caught between the Croc and Gucci City.

269 International Crisis Group, 'Zimbabwe's "military-assisted transition" and prospects for recovery', p. 4.

270 Raftopoulos, Caught between the Croc and Gucci City.

271 New York Times, 'Robert Mugabe, in speech to Zimbabwe, refused to say if he will resign', 11.11.17.

272 International Crisis Group, 'Zimbabwe's "military-assisted transition" and prospects for recovery', p. 4.

273 Herald, 'President resigns!', 22.11.17.

Mugabe's long-awaited downfall prompted exuberant celebrations in the streets of Zimbabwe's urban centres.[274] Zimbabwe's de facto coup was thus reminiscent of the removal of Egyptian President Mohamed Morsi by the military, which equally enjoyed popular support, even though it constituted a flagrant breach of the fundamental constitutional principles that consolidated authoritarian rule in the name of stability. To provide a legal veneer for the coup and the forthcoming inauguration of Mnangagwa as interim president (although he was no longer vice president), the High Court overturned Mugabe's decision to fire Mnangagwa, and ruled that the army's intervention did not violate the constitution. This indicated, as Zambara highlights, that the judiciary would continue to operate on the whims of the executive, as it did during the Mugabe era.[275]

Indeed, the coup marked a historic caesura, in that it ended Mugabe's 37-year rule at the helm of the state; but in fact it perpetuated the authoritarian system of governance of the ZANU-PF regime, of which the military had always been part and parcel.[276] After being inaugurated as president, Mnangagwa – who had been one of the principle architects of Zimbabwe's security state and, alongside the military, responsible for the human rights abuses of the post-independence era – appointed his old comrades from ZANU-PF's inner circle of power to cabinet. Moreover, he appointed General Chiwenga as his deputy president, Air Marshal Perence Shiri as minister of lands, agriculture and rural settlements, and Major General Sibusiso Moyo as minister of foreign affairs.[277]

The coup also helped to consolidate the ZANU-PF regime, because Mugabe had long become a liability both domestically and internationally. ZANU-PF stood a better chance of winning the forthcoming 2018 elections without having to use excessive violence or intimidation once the intractable succession struggle had been settled, the 93-year-old was no longer standing for re-election, and the supremacy of the military had been spectacularly demonstrated. The removal of the polarising figure of Mugabe, who continued to be subject to Western sanctions and emblematically stood for the Zimbabwean pariah state, was likely to facilitate re-engagement with international donors and, possibly, investors. The widespread perception that Mugabe was the problem and that he needed to go is likely to have contributed to the international acquiescence with the de facto coup that swept the autocrat from power.

SADC had watched Zimbabwe's renewed descent into crisis after the 2013 elections and, just like the AU and the wider international community, did little in response to the military-induced change of leadership. For 13 years, SADC had sought to contain the unfolding Zimbabwean crisis through a range of diplomatic initiatives; after the GPA process (of which SADC was the guarantor) had consumed so much of SADC's attention at the expense of other issues of regional development, the sufficient-

---

274 Eppel, Shari, 'Harare – The morning after', SPT Brief, Cape Town, Solidarity Peace Trust, 21 November 2017.

275 Webster Zambara, interview via email, 10.12.17.

276 Sabelo Ndlovu-Gatsheni, interview via Skype, 2.12.17.

277 Southall, 'Bob's out, the Croc is in: Continuity or change in Zimbabwe?,' pp. 74–76.

ly credible 2013 elections had provided the Summit with an opportunity to rid itself of the perennial Zimbabwean problem for the time being.[278] The imperative of anti-imperialist resistance, solidarity among liberation party governments, the high regard for the struggle icon, Mugabe, and a reluctance to intervene in the domestic affairs of member states to enforce democratic SADC principles remained the underlying principles that guided the region's policy vis-à-vis the unresolved Zimbabwean crisis in the post-GPA period.[279] Since the region was weary of the perennial succession struggle (and of Mugabe), and since SADC had, as Raftopoulos emphasises, long regarded a reformed ZANU-PF government without Mugabe as the most desirable outcome of a transition, the region was willing to accept the military-induced transfer of power, so long as the coup leaders maintained a pretence of constitutionality.[280]

As the coup unfolded, the SADC Organ Troika Ministerial Committee convened a meeting and the SADC chair, Jacob Zuma, issued a statement expressing SADC's concern.[281] Besides calling on the government and army to resolve the 'political impasse' amicably, SADC expressed 'hope that developments in Zimbabwe would not lead to unconstitutional changes of government, as that would be contrary to both SADC and African Union principles'.[282] While South African envoys held talks with Mugabe and army officials, the SADC chair cancelled a visit to Harare after meeting Mnangagwa in Pretoria.[283] It is likely that by this point, SADC leaders condoned Mugabe's removal by the army, provided the forced transfer of power could be made to appear constitutional. The military's intervention, Ndlovu-Gatsheni suggests, may also have been sanctioned by Zimbabwe's most important international partner, China.[284] While thanking Mugabe for his service to the region and his merits as a liberation hero, SADC was quick to congratulate Mnangagwa on his inauguration as interim president.[285] SADC's handling of the coup reflected both its relative impotence vis-à-vis Zimbabwe's securocrats and its unwillingness to uphold its democratic principles at a high cost. But the acquiescence to the coup that further entrenched the securocrats in civilian governance set a dangerous precedent for both Zimbabwe and the region, signalling that unconstitutional changes of government and military meddling were tolerated by SADC, if they were thinly disguised in constitutional terms.

278 Aeby, 'Zimbabwe's gruelling transition', p. 300.

279 Sabelo Ndlovu-Gatsheni, interview via Skype, 2.12.17.

280 Raftopoulos, Caught between the Croc and Gucci City.

281 SADC, Press Release: SADC Organ Troika Plus Council Chairperson Ministerial Meeting discusses the Political Situation in Zimbabwe, 16.11.17.

282 SADC, SADC Statement on the unfolding events in the Republic of Zimbabwe by H.E Jacob Zuma, President of the Republic of South Africa and Chairperson of SADC, Pretoria, 15.11.17.

283 EWN Eyewitness News, 'Zuma holds off on Zim visit after meeting Mnangagwa', 22.11.17; Financial Times, 'South Africa envoys meet Mugabe in bid to end Zimbabwe's crisis', 16.11.17.

284 Sabelo Ndlovu-Gatsheni, interview via Skype, 2.12.17.

285 SADC Executive Secretary H. E. Stergomena Lawerence Tax, SADC Congratulates his Excellency Emmerson Dambudzo Mnangagwa, President of the Republic of Zimbabwe, 24.11.17.

Zimbabwe since the coup: Elections, protests and violent repression

The negative political and economic trends in Zimbabwe have not been reversed since the coup (when the above analysis was written). Zimbabwe's 2018 elections were mired in post-electoral violence; the security apparatus of the Mnangagwa government cracked down on opponents; and rapid price hikes put further pressure on vulnerable households.

Having assumed office in a dubious transition of power, the Mnangagwa-led government set out to restore its legitimacy in the July 2018 general elections and to attract international investment to kickstart the economy. In the run-up to the elections, ZANU-PF, therefore, promulgated liberal economic policies under the mantra 'Zimbabwe is open for business'; invoked a language of peace and reconciliation vis-à-vis white farmers; and enabled selective electoral reforms, so that the elections would be internationally accepted.[286] The piecemeal reforms included the introduction of an electoral court to process petitions, a code of conduct for contestants, and a 10% threshold for the printing of ballot papers in excess of the registered voting population. The independence of the ZEC, however, remained in question, even though its chair resigned ahead of the poll. A new electoral roll was used, following a biometric voter registration process that was embraced for the first time in Zimbabwe; but the registration process was tainted by reports of intimidation, and the electoral roll still lacked transparency. To boost international confidence in the process, previously excluded observers were invited to monitor the elections, including observers from the European Union, the Commonwealth and the International Republican Institute. International and civil society observers found that the electoral playing field remained uneven, but that the pre-election environment and the voting process were generally peaceful and orderly. An explosion at a rally of the ZANU-PF candidate, Mnangagwa, however, injured several party officials. The media remained polarised in the campaign period, with ZANU-PF receiving the bulk of the national broadcaster's election coverage.[287]

The presidential election – which was contested by 23 candidates – was not only the first without Mugabe since independence; it was also the first without the late Morgan Tsvangirai in the two decades since the MDC was formed.[288] Although it had formed an MDC Alliance, the fragmented opposition went into the election divided, having undergone a protracted leadership struggle, from which Tsvangirai's anointed successor, Nelson Chamisa, had emerged as party leader.[289]

Conflict erupted after the poll, when the MDC Alliance declared victory before the official results were announced and alleged that ZANU-PF had colluded with the ZEC to rig the elections. On 1 August, at least seven people, including bystanders, were killed during opposition protests in Harare, when police and soldiers fired live

---

286 Solidarity Peace Trust, Zimbabwe: The 2018 elections and their aftermath (Cape Town, 2018), pp. 3–10.

287 Zimbabwe Election Support Network, Report on the 30th July 2018 Harmonised Elections (Harare, 2018), pp. 11–16.

288 Zimbabwe Election Support Network, Report on the 30th July 2018 Harmonised Elections, pp. 11–16.

289 Solidarity Peace Trust, Zimbabwe: The 2018 elections and their aftermath, pp. 3–10.

ammunition, using unjustified and disproportionate force, as a commission of inquiry would confirm.[290] According to the official results (which the MDC Alliance unsuccessfully challenged in court), Mnangagwa won the presidential election with 50.6% of the vote, while Chamisa received 44.3%. ZANU-PF also won 144 seats in the National Assembly, while the MDC Alliance obtained 64 seats.[291] While the Mnangagwa government could entrench and legitimise its hold on power, the violent crackdown on protesters yet again illustrated the authoritarian and militaristic character of its rule, casting doubt on its willingness to accept democratic rights and principles.

As the economic situation deteriorated throughout 2018, the price of basic commodities increased rapidly, the country experienced a severe petrol shortage, cholera broke out in Harare, and the fragile livelihood of the majority of Zimbabweans became even more precarious. In late 2018, public sector workers, who represent 27.4% of the remaining formal work force, went on strike to protest about their working conditions and their salaries, which were affected by rising inflation and a persistent monetary crisis. A 250% increase in petrol prices announced by the president in January 2019 sparked a new wave of protests that turned violent as urban areas witnessed the anger and frustration of unemployed youth, who looted shops and destroyed property. As the army and police cracked down brutally on the protests, 17 people were reportedly killed and over 950 arrested. The state security apparatus used the opportunity to clamp down on civil society, arresting the leaders of prominent human rights and pro-democracy groups. Mnangagwa's invitation to a 'national dialogue' that would, however, only include political parties, rang hollow in the face of the violent clampdown by the unreconstructed authoritarian ZANU-PF regime.[292]

SADC responded to the renewed escalation of violent conflict and state repression by adopting the stance of the Mnangagwa government, which blamed civil society for the upheaval, and routinely condemned international sanctions.[293] Two decades into the Zimbabwe crisis, SADC thus had yet to find an effective response to the enduring authoritarianism and poor governance in Zimbabwe that continued to hold back the development of the Southern African community as a whole.

290 AP NEWS, 'Zimbabwe inquiry finds army, police killed 6 during protest', 18.12.18; Zimbabwe Election Support Network, Report on the 30th July 2018 Harmonised Elections, pp. 11–16.

291 Solidarity Peace Trust, Zimbabwe: The 2018 elections and their aftermath, pp. 3–10.

292 Solidarity Peace Trust, Resurgent Authoritarianism: The politics of the January 2019 violence in Zimbabwe (Cape Town, 2019), pp. 2–6.

293 Solidarity Peace Trust, Resurgent Authoritarianism, pp. 2–6.

Southern Africa is likely to experience more social unrest in the foreseeable future.

Chapter 5, page 83

Two men cleaning a window in an office building in Maputo, Mozambique, May 2011. Photo: Nina May, Flickr.

5. Conclusion

The purpose of this report has been to provide an overview of political and economic developments in Southern Africa that are relevant to regional peace and security. The above discussion has, therefore, highlighted challenges relating to armed conflict, crises of governance and socio-economic development deficits, and these aspects have been discussed in greater detail for the cases of Mozambique, Angola and Zimbabwe. Moreover, the study has reviewed the development of SADC's institutional framework for peace and security, its guiding policy principles and selected crisis responses. The above discussion underlines that, while the region continues to experience isolated armed conflicts, and while developmental backlogs present a major risk to regional stability in the long run, currently the most acute source of instability stems from governance deficits, which in the past decade have prompted crises in a variety of SADC states. Although SADC has gradually established a peace and security infrastructure in line with the APSA, the institutions have little capacity: they lack material and political support, as member states are reluctant to cede authority to supranational structures or to enforce SADC principles. SADC's liberal-democratic norms are, in practice, overridden by imperatives of anti-imperialism, stability and regime solidarity, and SADC has not been able to respond effectively to either of the recent intrastate crises discussed. The governance deficits highlighted and SADC's lacklustre conflict management may arrest the development of the Southern African region in the long run.

The discussion has illustrated the fact that, while Southern Africa has gradually evolved from being a region riddled by large-scale wars (which in several instances outlasted the Cold War and the apartheid era), the region continues to grapple with isolated armed conflicts, governance deficits and economic disparities that are rooted in the region's violent colonial and post-colonial past. In contrast to the intertwined wars against white minority regimes during the Cold War and the Congo wars, contemporary conflicts in Southern Africa are overwhelmingly of a national rather than an international nature.[294] Besides the ongoing war against multiple armed groups in eastern DRC, minor armed conflicts have been reignited in Mozambique and Angola. RENAMO rebels took up arms in 2012 and, although they lack the military capability to restart a civil war, they have attacked government troops and transport routes, causing economic disruption and insecurity. The insurgency, which was driven by the rebel leader's political ambitions and the social grievances of marginalised fighters, enabled RENAMO to compel the government to concede territorial autonomies, political privileges and economic benefits in negotiations. While a truce brought a halt to violent hostilities, the peace will remain fragile, so long as grievances relating to authoritarian and centralised governance and economic marginalisation are not addressed, RENAMO fighters are not demobilised and the ambitions of its leader are

294 Africa and Molomo, 'Security in southern Africa', p. 58.

not contained.[295] Moreover, a series of brutal attacks by a militant Islamist group in northern Mozambique in 2018 raised fears that violent religious extremism could take root in Southern Africa.[296] In Angola, separatist insurgents have continued to attack government troops in oil-rich Cabinda and have disrupted extractive activities. The enduring low-scale insurgency arguably does not have the potential to destabilise the Angolan state, but it has allowed the MPLA government to maintain a tight security clampdown on Cabinda and, by extension, the country.[297]

As the discussion has illustrated, the most acute crises in SADC states in the past 10 years have been prompted by matters of governance, including electoral stalemates, authoritarian rule, government unaccountability and the abuse of state resources for the preservation of power. While these crises and governance deficits have not exclusively affected states governed by liberation parties, the discussion has drawn on recent scholarly debates to show that some of these challenges are fostered by liberation movement and guerrilla army legacies. The war-time socialisation of political elites accounts to a considerable extent for the continued authoritarian traits, lack of democratic values, commando style of governance and militaristic culture of several Southern African governments, as well as for the involvement of the security sector in civilian affairs and party politics. In some instances, liberation party elites took control of the oppressive instruments they inherited from the settler state, and have continued to use these to crush opponents, entrench themselves in power and accumulate wealth. Moreover, both the political and military elites that had dedicated themselves to the armed struggle against racist regimes, and the political organisations that saw themselves as Leninist vanguard parties developed a sense of entitlement to power and privilege.[298]

These tendencies have been most pronounced in Zimbabwe, where the ZANU-PF regime equates the loss of state power to a reversal of the country's liberation from colonialism, and where the military leadership has portrayed its coup as an operation to protect the liberation legacy.[299] But the trend could equally well be observed in Mozambique, where the FRELIMO government's liberation narrative has left an imprint on the post-war nation-building project, making it difficult for party stalwarts to accept political opposition and freedom of expression.[300] The prevalent political culture in Angola that was shaped during decades of war leaves little space for the political competition that is needed for a democratic society, and this has become manifest in a coercive 'command state' that has enabled a kleptocratic elite to virtually monopolise the country's national resources.[301]

---

295 Elísio Macamo, interview, Basel, 22.11.17; Vines, 'Renamo's rise and decline', pp. 386–88.

296 Fabricius, 'Mozambique's apparent Islamist insurgency poses multiple threats'.

297 Didier Péclard, interview via email, 8.12.17.

298 Elísio Macamo, interview, Basel, 22.11.17; Sabelo Ndlovu-Gatsheni, interview via Skype, 2.12.17; Didier Péclard, interview via email, 8.12.17; Melber, 'Struggle mentality versus democracy', pp. 143–56; Ranger, 'Nationalist historiography, patriotic history and the history of the nation', pp. 215–34.

299 Herald, 'The operation to restore legacy', 5.12.17; Raftopoulos, Caught between the Croc and Gucci City.

300 Macamo, 'Violence and political culture in Mozambique', pp. 85–100.

301 Ingles, 'The MPLA government', pp. 45–55.

However, the liberation party governments of South Africa and Namibia are among the most democratic states in the region and – although they have displayed some of these tendencies – they have generally adhered to the principles of liberal electoral democracy. Although most SADC states have undergone a transition from authoritarian to democratic regime types, the level of democratisation in the SADC region continues to vary widely, ranging from closed and electoral authoritarian systems to electoral and liberal democracies; over the past two decades, they have taken contrasting trajectories that are neither linear nor irreversible.[302] While democracy is neither a guarantee of nor a prerequisite for peace and stability, the democratic deficits, poor governance and lack of accountability that bedevil even some of the most democratic SADC states have, in the past two decades, accounted for a whole range of intrastate crises encompassing elections, change of government, mismanagement of public affairs and disregard for citizens' aspirations.[303] Currently, governance deficits constitute the most immediate threat to peace and security in Southern Africa.

Southern Africa features some of the world's most unequal societies, characterised by enormous social cleavages that were shaped by settler colonialism and racial segregation, and that have been sustained in the post-colonial period. It is therefore unsurprising that socio-economic grievances should not only impinge on human security, but also represent a formidable challenge to peace and stability in the region in the long term. Investments in human capital and the creation of economic opportunities have been impeded by sluggish growth rates, and unemployment has been rising steadily across much of the region over the past decade. Vast swathes of the population continue to live under the respective national poverty line in virtually all SADC countries, and several consecutive years of drought and extreme weather conditions – phenomena that are likely to become more frequent, owing to climate change – have exposed vulnerable communities to acute food shortages.[304]

In the absence of improved economic and educational opportunities for its rapidly growing young population (34.2% of the region's population are under the age of 25), Southern Africa is likely to experience more social unrest in the foreseeable future.[305] In South Africa, the social protests that are fuelled by continued inequities in the country have, in many instances, turned violent and have prompted a violent response by the post-apartheid state.[306] In Angola, rampant inequality and the flagrant accumulation of wealth by the ruling elites have prompted youth protests against the government, which has responded with violence and repression.[307] Similarly, economic despair and frustration with a complacent and corrupt government gave rise to a new

302 Matlosa, 'The state of democratisation in Southern Africa', pp. 5–7.

303 International Crisis Group, Crisis Watch Database, 30.9.17.

304 SADC, SADC Regional Vulnerability Assessment, p. 9; SADC, Statistical Yearbook 2015, http://www.sadc.int/information-services/sadc-statistics

305 SADC, SADC Regional Vulnerability Assessment, p. 9.

306 Mkhize, 'Is South Africa's 20 years of democracy in crisis?', pp. 190–206; Perez Nino and Le Billon, 'Foreign aid', pp. 79–96; Vines et al., 'Mozambique to 2018', p. 14.

307 Didier Péclard, interview via email, 8.12.17.

wave of protest movements in Zimbabwe.[308] Moreover, the discussion has shown that in Mozambique, economic grievances and a feeling of marginalisation have prompted social unrest in the capital and have enabled political entrepreneurs to mobilise fighters for the RENAMO rebellion; meanwhile, the award of licences allowing the politically connected elites to exploit the country's mineral wealth leaves the population feeling short-changed, which has the potential to generate further conflict.[309]

The study has also sought to assess SADC's preparedness to respond effectively to peace and security challenges in its member states. To this end, the discussion above outlined the development of SADC's institutional framework and policies. The institutional legacies of SADC's predecessor organisations led to a preoccupation with national sovereignty and a bifurcated structure that initially vested the Summit and Organ with authority to manage peace and security concerns. SADC's small Secretariat and directorate of the Organ remain poorly resourced, and institutions of the SADC Treaty – such as the Parliamentary Forum and the SADC Tribunal – have never been fully actualised (or dismantled), owing to member states' unwillingness to cede authority to these supranational structures, which could potentially protect the rights of citizens against arbitrary rule.[310]

The lifespan of SADC's most important policy document on peace and security, SIPO II, has been extended to 2020, although it is outdated in parts and fails to offer concrete and workable plans to achieve its numerous stated objectives.[311] In terms of SIPO II's implementation, progress has been made with regard to election management, the establishment of a mediation infrastructure, SADC's peace-keeping and early warning capacities, and the regional coordination of police and crime fighting.[312] Implementation of the plan and functioning of the infrastructure have, however, been impeded by a lack of coordination between SADC institutions and, most importantly, by member states' unwillingness to give adequate material and political support to the supranational structures that were created on the initiative of the Secretariat and donors. While SADC has thus established all sub-regional components of the continental APSA, including a Standby Force whose readiness for deployment has been demonstrated in the DRC and Lesotho, most of the institutions, especially those in the critical domain of mediation and preventive diplomacy, function poorly and are short-staffed.[313]

The normative guidelines in SADC's policies on regional peace and security entail inherent tensions between the principles of national sovereignty on the one hand, and

308 Aeby and Chitanga, 'Transforming an agrarian state with hashtags?', p. 7.

309 Hofmann, 'Mozambique's economic transformation', pp. 102–16; Nogueira et al., 'Mozambican economic porosity', p. 114; Elísio Macamo, interview, Basel, 22.11.17.

310 Cawthra, The Role of SADC, p. 11; Hendricks and Musavengana, The Security Sector in Southern Africa, p. 31; International Crisis Group, Implementing Peace and Security Architecture (II), p. 7; Nathan, 'Solidarity triumphs', p. 131.

311 Anthoni Van Nieuwkerk, interview via email, Johannesburg, 12.12.17; Van Nieuwkerk, 'Exploring', p. 47; van Nieuwkerk, 'SIPO II: Too little, too late?', p. 150.

312 Anthoni Van Nieuwkerk, interview via email, Johannesburg, 12.12.17.

313 Aeby, 'Stability and sovereignty', p. 273; Laurie Nathan, interview by email, 2.12.17; Anthoni Van Nieuwkerk, interview via email, Johannesburg, 12.12.17.

SADC's mandate to promote peace, human rights and democracy in member states on the other. In practice, the principles that give guidance to SADC crisis responses are renegotiated by the heterogeneous membership of the Summit. Stability and sovereignty tend to take precedence over democracy, owing to the dominance of liberation party governments, the lack of democratic commitment by some members, and SADC's limited capacity to enforce its principles against non-compliant regimes. The region's anti-imperialist defence reaction, which has been exploited by Zimbabwe and other regimes, has prevented the effective protection of human security by SADC.[314]

SADC reacted dramatically to military meddling in civilian politics and government instability in the tiny state of Lesotho, by sanctioning the deployment of troops; and several SADC states contributed troop contingents to the UN-mandated Force Intervention Brigade in the DRC, where they suffered human losses. SADC was, however, unable to respond effectively either to the political crisis created by DRC President Kabila's failure to hold elections before his constitutional term of office expired, or to the intrastate crises in Angola, Mozambique and Zimbabwe discussed above.[315] Given that the formerly apartheid-sponsored RENAMO enjoyed little sympathy among Southern Africa's liberation party governments, SADC was, understandably, in no position to act as a credible and impartial mediator in the Mozambican conflict. However, the organisation also omitted to respond either to the rebellion in Cabinda or to the state-sponsored violence in Angola.[316] After 13 years of trying to contain the Zimbabwean crisis through a series of diplomatic initiatives, SADC watched Zimbabwe's renewed descent into economic and political crisis after the SADC-brokered power-sharing process ended and the severely flawed, yet sufficiently credible, 2013 election allowed the Summit to drop the perennial Zimbabwean problem from its agenda for the time being. Although it was stressed that neither the AU nor SADC would tolerate an unconstitutional change of government, a thin veneer of constitutionality allowed SADC and the international community to acquiesce to the de facto military coup that compelled President Mugabe to resign and that entrenched in government those ZANU-PF's military hardliners who were responsible for most of the human rights abuses of the post-colonial period. By accepting the coup, SADC not only displayed its impotence vis-à-vis the securocrats and its unwillingness to enforce democratic principles at a high cost, but also set a dangerous precedent by signalling that the Community would tolerate unconstitutional changes of government and military meddling, provided they were thinly disguised in constitutional terms. As Zimbabwe continues to spiral into political and socio-economic crisis in the post-Mugabe era, SADC has yet to find an effective response to the enduring authoritarianism and poor governance that continue to retard the development of the Southern African community of states.

---

314 Aeby, 'Stability and sovereignty', p. 273; Nathan, Community of Insecurity, pp. 23–25.

315 SADC, Executive Secretary Stergomena Lawrence Tax, SADC Congratulates His Excellency Emmerson Dambudzo Mnangagwa, President of the Republic of Zimbabwe, Gaborone, 24.11.17; SADC, Organ Troika Communiqué, Luanda, 21.11.17; SADC, Summit Communiqué, Pretoria, 20.8.17; SADC, SADC Executive Secretary Condemns Attack on Tanzania Peacekeepers, Gaborone, 9.12.17.

316 Roque, Reform or Unravel?, p. 5.

About the author

Michael Aeby is an Associated Researcher at the Institute for Democracy, Citizenship and Public Policy in Africa (IDCPPA), University of Cape Town. His research focuses on civil society participation in peace processes, mediation, intergovernmental organisations, peace agreement implementation, transitional governance and, power-sharing. His geographical expertise relates to the Southern African Development Community region, in particular, Zimbabwe.

Michael Aeby holds a PhD and MA from the University of Basel, where he specialised in African history and peace research, and a BA in history from the University of Fribourg. Before joining the University of Cape Town, he worked at the Graduate Institute in Geneva and the Statehood Programme of Swisspeace. He was a visiting fellow at the universities of the Witwatersrand, Western Cape and Zimbabwe and interned the South African Human Science Research Council.

Below is an incomplete list of Michael Aeby's previous contributions to books, peer-reviewed scientific journals and other publications:

- 'Inside the Inclusive Government', Interparty Dynamics in Zimbabwe's Power -Sharing Executive, *The Journal of Southern African Studies,* 44/5, (2018), 855-877.
- Women in Peace & Transition Processes: South Africa's Democratic Transition (1990–1998), Inclusive Peace & Transition Initiative, Graduate Institute of International Development Studies, Geneva, November 2018.
- Peace & Security Challenges in Southern Africa: Governance Deficits and Lacklustre Regional Conflict Management, *Policy Note* N° 4:18, Nordic Africa Institute, Uppsala, May 2018.
- 'Stability and Sovereignty at the Expense of Democracy? The SADC Mediation Mandate for Zimbabwe, 2007 – 13', *African Security,* 10/3-4 (2017), pp 272-291.
- 'Making an Impact from the Margins? Civil Society Groups in Zimbabwe's Interim Power-Sharing Process', *The Journal of Modern African Studies,* 54/4 (2016), pp 703-28.

References

Scholarly works

Aeby, Michael, 'Zimbabwe's gruelling transition: Interim power-sharing and conflict management in Southern Africa', University of Basel, 2015.

Aeby, Michael, 'Making an impact from the margins? Civil society groups in Zimbabwe's interim power-sharing process', *Journal of Modern African Studies*, 54, 4 (2016), pp. 703–28.

Aeby, Michael, 'Stability and sovereignty at the expense of democracy? The SADC mediation mandate for Zimbabwe, 2007–2013', *African Security*, 10, 3–4 (2017), pp. 272–91.

Aeby, Michael and Chitanga, Gideon, 'Transforming an agrarian state with hashtags? Urban civil society and the quest for state transformation in Zimbabwe (2013–17)', paper presented at the 7th European Conference on African Studies, University of Basel, 30.6.17.

Africa, Sandy and Molomo, Mpho, 'Security in southern Africa: The state of the debate', in A. Van Nieuwkerk and K. Hofmann (eds), *Southern African Security Review 2013* (Maputo, Friedrich Ebert Stiftung, 2013), pp. 13–26.

Andreasson, Stefan, 'Confronting the settler legacy: Indigenisation and transformation in South Africa and Zimbabwe', *Political Geography*, 29, 8 (2010), pp. 424–33.

Arthur, Peter, 'Promoting security in Africa through regional economic communities (RECs) and the African Union's African Peace and Security Architecture (APSA)', *Insight on Africa*, 9, 1 (2017), pp. 1–21.

Bereketeab, Redie, 'Introduction: Understanding national liberation movements', in R. Bereketeab (ed.), *National Liberation Movements as Government in Africa* (Abingdon, Routledge, 2017), pp. 1–15.

Birmingham, David, 'Angola', in P. Chabal (ed.), *A History of Postcolonial Lusophone Africa* (London, Indiana University Press, 2002), pp. 137–84.

Bond, Patrick, 'The African National Congress: From liberation movement to neoliberal state manager', in R. Bereketeab (ed.), *National Liberation Movements as Government in Africa* (Abingdon, Routledge, 2017), pp. 107–21.

Bourne, Richard, *Catastrophe: What went wrong in Zimbabwe?* (London and New York, Zed Books, 2011).

Bruce, David. 'Political Killings in South Africa'. Policy Brief. Pretoria: *Institute for Security Studies, 2014*. https://issafrica.s3.amazonaws.com/site/uploads/PolBrief64.pdf.

Catholic Commission for Justice and Peace in Zimbabwe, *Breaking the Silence, Building True Peace: A report on the disturbances in Matabeleland & the Midlands 1980–88* (Harare, 1999).

Cawthra, Gavin, *The Role of SADC in Managing Political Crisis and Conflict: The cases of Madagascar and Zimbabwe* (Maputo, Friedrich Ebert Stiftung, 2011).

Cawthra, Gavin, 'The role of donors and NGOs in the security policy process in southern Africa', in A. Van Nieuwkerk and K. Hofmann (eds), *Southern African Security Review 2013* (Maputo, Friedrich Ebert Stiftung, 2013), pp. 27–37.

Chan, Stephen, *Robert Mugabe: A Life of Power and Violence* (London, I.B. Tauris, 2003).

Chan, Stephen, and Ranka Primorac. 'Postscript: Making Do in Hybrid House.' In *Zimbabwe Since the Unity Government*, Stephen Chan and Ranka Primorac (eds.), New York, Routledge, 2013, pp. 119–23.

Chikane, Frank, *Eight Days in September: The removal of Thabo Mbeki* (Johannesburg, Picador Africa, 2012).

Chipkin, Ivor, 'The decline of African nationalism and the state of South Africa', *Journal of Southern African Studies*, 42, 2 (2016), pp. 215–27.

Chung, Fay, *Re-Living the Second Chimurenga: Memories from the liberation struggle in Zimbabwe* (Harare, Weaver Press, 2006).

Cole, Rowland J.V., 'Power-sharing, post-electoral contestations and the dismemberment of the right to democracy in Africa', *International Journal of Human Rights*, 17, 2 (2013), pp. 256–74.

Curtis, Devon, 'South Africa: "Exporting Peace" to the Great Lakes Region?', in A. Adebajo, A. Adedeji and C. Landsberg (eds), *South Africa in Africa: The post-apartheid era* (Pietermaritzburg, University of KZN Press, 2007), pp. 253–73.

Darch, Colin, 'Separatist tensions and violence in the "model post-conflict state": Mozambique since the 1990s', *Review of African Political Economy*, 43, 148 (2016), pp. 320–27.

Dawson, Martin and Kelsall, Tim, 'Anti-developmental patrimonialism in Zimbabwe', *Journal of Contemporary African Studies*, 30, 1 (2012), pp. 49–66.

De Jager, Nicola and Steenekamp, Cindy Lee, 'The changing political culture of the African National Congress', *Democratization*, 23, 5 (2016), pp. 919–39.

Dorman, Sara Rich, *Understanding Zimbabwe: From liberation to authoritarianism* (London: Hurst & Company, 2016).

Eppel, Shari, 'Harare – The morning after', SPT Brief, Cape Town, Solidarity Peace Trust, 21 November 2017.

Fabricius, Peter, 'Could Afonso Dhlakama's death bring permanent peace to Mozambique?, ISS Today, 11.5.18.

Fabricius, Peter, 'Mozambique's first Islamist attacks shock the region: A new armed group calling itself al-Shabaab is spreading fear in a usually jihad-free region', *ISS Today*, Institute for Security Studies, 27.10.17.

Fabricius, Peter, 'Mozambique's apparent Islamist insurgency poses multiple threats', ISS Today, 20.11.18.

Ganho, Ana, 'The murder of Gilles Cistac: Mozambique's future at a crossroads', *Review of African Political Economy*, 43, 147 (2016), pp. 142–50.

Guimarães, Fernando Andresen, *The Origins of the Angolan Civil War: Foreign intervention and domestic conflict* (London and New York, Macmillan/St Martin's Press, 1998).

Hanlon, Joseph, 'Following the donor-designed path to Mozambique's US$2.2 billion secret debt deal', *Third World Quarterly*, 38, 3 (2017), pp. 753–70.

Hendricks, Cheryl and Musavengana, Takawira (eds), *The Security Sector in Southern Africa* (Pretoria, Institute for Security Studies, 2010).

Hodges, Tony, *Angola: From Afro-Stalinism to petro-diamond capitalism* (Oxford and Bloomington, James Currey/Indiana University Press, 2001).

Hoffmann, Kasper, Vlassenroot, Koen and Marchais, Gauthier, 'Taxation, stateness and armed groups: Public authority and resource extraction in eastern Congo', *Development and Change*, 47, 6 (2016), p. 1434.

Hofmann, Katharina, 'Mozambique's economic transformation and its implications for human security', in A. Van Nieuwkerk and K. Hofmann (eds), *Southern African Security Review 2013* (Maputo, Friedrich Ebert Stiftung, 2013), pp. 102–19.

Holanda Maschietto, Roberta, 'Decentralisation and local governance in Mozambique: The challenges of promoting bottom-up dynamics from the top down', *Conflict, Security & Development*, 16, 2 (2016).

Human Rights Watch, *Perpetual Fear: Impunity and cycles of violence in Zimbabwe* (New York, 2011).

Ingles, Paulo, 'The MPLA government and its post-liberation record in Angola', in R. Bereketeab (ed.), *National Liberation Movements as Government in Africa* (Abingdon, Routledge, 2017), pp. 41–55.

International Crisis Group, 'Resistance and denial: Zimbabwe's stalled reform agenda', *Africa Briefing* (16 November 2011).

International Crisis Group, *Implementing Peace and Security Architecture (II): Southern Africa* (Johannesburg, 2012).

International Crisis Group, *Zimbabwe's Sanctions Standoff* (Johannesburg, 2012).

International Crisis Group, 'Zimbabwe's "military-assisted transition" and prospects for recovery', *Africa Briefing* (20 December 2017).

Kabemba, Claude, 'South Africa and the DRC: Is a stable and developmental state possible in the Congo?', in S. Roger (ed.), *South Africa's Role in Conflict Resolution and Peacemaking in Africa* (Cape Town, HSRC Press, 2006), pp. 151–72.

Kagwanja, Peter, 'Power and peace: South Africa and the refurbishing of Africa's multilateral capacity for peacemaking', in R. Southall (ed.), *South Africa's Role in Conflict Resolution and Peacemaking in Africa* (Cape Town, HSRC Press, 2006).

Kanyenze, Godfrey, Kondo, Timothy, Chitambara, Prosper and Martens, Jos, *Beyond the Enclave: Towards a pro-poor and inclusive development strategy for Zimbabwe* (Harare, Weaver Press/LEDRIZ, 2011).

Khadiagala, Gilbert M., 'The SADCC and its approaches to African regionalism', in C. Saunders, G.A. Dzinesa and D. Nagar (eds), *Region-Building in Southern Africa: Progress, problems and prospects* (London, Zed Books, 2012), pp. 25–38.

Kriger, Norma, 'ZANU PF politics under Zimbabwe's "power-sharing" government', *Journal of Contemporary African Studies*, 30, 1 (2012), pp. 11–26.

Le Billon, Philippe, 'Oil and armed conflicts in Africa', *African Geographical Review*, 29, 1 (2010), pp. 63–90.

Lins De Albuquerque, Adriana and Hull Wiklund, Cecilia, *Challenges to Peace and Security in Southern Africa: The role of SADC* (Stockholm, Swedish Defence Research Agency, 2015). https://www.foi.se/download/18.7fd35d7f166c56ebe0bb390/1542369060270/Challenges-to-Peace-and-Security-in-S-Africa_The-Role-of-SADC_FOI-Memo-5594.pdf

Macamo, Elísio, 'Violence and political culture in Mozambique', *Social Dynamics*, 42, 1 (2016), pp. 85–105.

Macamo, Elísio, 'Power, conflict, and citizenship: Mozambique's contemporary struggles', *Citizenship Studies*, 21, 2 (2017), pp. 196–209.

Magure, Booker, 'Foreign investment, black economic empowerment and militarised patronage politics in Zimbabwe', *Journal of Contemporary African Studies*, 30, 1 (2012), pp. 67–82.

Masunungure, Eldred V., 'A militarized election: The 27 June presidential run-off', in E.V. Masunungure (ed.), *Defying the Winds of Change: Zimbabwe's 2008 elections* (Harare, Weaver Press, 2009), pp. 79–97.

Mandaza, Ibbo. 'Will ZANU PF Survive After Mugabe?', In *The Day After Mugabe*, Gugulethu Moyo and Mark Ashurst (eds.), (London, Africa Research Institute, 2007), 39–45.

Matlosa, Khabele, *Consolidating Democratic Governance in the SADC Region: Transitions and prospects for consolidation* (Johannesburg, EISA, 2008).

Matlosa, Khabele, 'Elections and conflict management', in C. Saunders, G.A. Dzinesa and D. Nagar (eds), *Region-Building in Southern Africa: Progress, problems and prospects* (London, Zed Books, 2012), pp. 78–91.

Matlosa, Khabele, 'The state of democratisation in Southern Africa: Blocked transitions, reversals, stagnation, progress and prospects', *Politikon*, 44, 1 (2017), pp. 5–26.

Matlosa, Khabele and Lotshwao, Kebapetse, *Political Integration and Democratisation in Southern Africa: Progress, problems and prospects* (Johannesburg, EISA, 2010).

Mazarire, Gerald, 'ZANU-PF and the government of national unity', in B. Raftopoulos (ed.), *The Hard Road to Reform* (Harare, Weaver Press, 2013), pp. 71–116.

Melber, Henning, 'Southern African liberation movements as governments and the limits to liberation', *Review of African Political Economy*, 36, 121 (2009), pp. 451–59.

Melber, Henning, 'Struggle mentality versus democracy: The case of SWAPO of Namibia', in R. Bereketeab (ed.), *National Liberation Movements as Government in Africa* (Abingdon, Routledge, 2017).

Mkhize, Mbekezeli C., 'Is South Africa's 20 years of democracy in crisis? Examining the impact of unrest incidents in local protests in the post-apartheid South Africa', *African Security Review*, 24, 2 (2015), pp. 190–206.

Mlambo, Alois S., 'The Zimbabwean crisis and international response', *Journal for Contemporary History*, 31 (2006), pp. 54–77.

Mlambo, Alois S., 'From an industrial powerhouse to a nation of vendors: Over two decades of economic decline and deindustrialization in Zimbabwe 1990–2015', *Journal of Developing Societies*, 33, 1 (2017), pp. 99–125.

Mtisi, Joseph, Nyakudya, Munyaradzi and Barnes, Teresa, 'War in Rhodesia, 1965–1980', in B. Raftopoulos and A. Mlambo (eds), *Becoming Zimbabwe: A history from the pre-colonial period to 2008* (Harare and Johannesburg, Weaver/Jacana, 2009).

Muzondidya, James, 'From buoyancy to crisis, 1980–1997', in B. Raftopoulos and A. Mlambo (eds), *Becoming Zimbabwe: A history from the pre-colonial period to 2008* (Harare and Johannesburg, Weaver/Jacana, 2009).

Nathan, Laurie, *Community of Insecurity: SADC's struggle for peace and security in Southern Africa* (Farnham, Ashgate Publishing, 2012).

Nathan, Laurie, 'Solidarity triumphs over democracy – the dissolution of the SADC Tribunal', *Development Dialogue*, 57 (2011), pp. 123–37.

Ndlovu-Gatsheni, Sabelo, 'Politics behind politics: African Union, SADC and the GPA in Zimbabwe', in B. Raftopoulos (ed.), *The Hard Road to Reform* (Harare, Weaver Press, 2013).

Ndlovu-Gatsheni, Sabelo, 'ZANU-PF in power in Zimbabwe, 1980–2013: Towards explaining why former liberation movements fail as governments', in R. Bereketeab (ed.), *National Liberation Movements as Government in Africa* (Abingdon, Routledge, 2017), pp. 122–40.

Nogueira, Isabela, Ollinaho, Ossi, Pinto, Eduardo Costa, Baruco, Grasiela, Saludjian, Alexis, Pinto, José Paulo Guedes, Balanco, Paulo and Schonerwald, Carlos, 'Mozambican economic porosity and the role of Brazilian capital: A political economy analysis', *Review of African Political Economy*, 44, 151 (2017), pp. 104–21.

Nuvunga, Adriano N., 'From former liberation movement to four decades in government: The maintenance of the Frelimo state', in R. Bereketeab (ed.), *National Liberation Movements as Government in Africa* (Abingdon, Routledge, 2017).

Nuvunga, Adriano N. and Eduardo, Sitoe, 'Party institutionalisation in Mozambique: "The party of the state" vs the opposition', *Journal of African Elections*, 12, 1 (2012), pp. 110–42.

Nyakudya, Munyaradzi, 'SADC's crisis management in Zimbabwe, 2007–2013', in Anthoni Van Nieuwkerk and Katharina Hofmann (eds), *Southern African Security Review 2013* (Maputo, Friedrich Ebert Stiftung, 2013).

Nyamunda, Tinashe, *Zimbabwe Bond Notes and Their Possible Long-term Legacy* (Harare, 2017).

Orre, Aslak, 'Covering up a massacre in Angola?', CHR Michelsen Institute, 19.5.15.

Ovadia, Jesse Salah, 'The dual nature of local content in Angola's oil and gas industry: Development vs elite accumulation', *Journal of Contemporary African Studies*, 30, 3 (2012), pp. 395–417.

Pearce, Justin, 'Youthful dissent challenges Angola's old elite', *Current History*, 115, 781 (2016), pp. 175–80.

Perez Nino, Helena and Le Billon, Philippe, 'Foreign aid, resource rents, and state fragility in Mozambique and Angola', *Annals of the American Academy of Political and Social Science*, 656, 1 (2014), pp. 79–96.

Phimister, Ian, 'The makings and meanings of the massacres in Matabeleland', *Development Dialogue*, 50 (2008), pp. 179–234.

Pigou, Piers, '*Standoff in Zimbabwe as Struggle to Succeed Mugabe Deepens*', Johannesburg: International Crisis Group, November 14, 2017.

Puddington, Arch and Roylance, Tyler, *Populists and Autocrats: The dual threat to global democracy* (Washington, DC, Freedom House, 2017).

Raftopoulos, Brian, 'Reflections on Opposition Politics in Zimbabwe: The Politics of the Movement for Democratic Change', *Reflections on Democratic Politics in Zimbabwe,* Brian Raftopoulos and Karin Alexander (eds.), (Cape Town, Institute for Justice and Reconciliation, 2006), pp. 6–28.

Raftopoulos, Brian, 'The labour movement and the emergence of opposition politics in Zimbabwe', *Labour, Capital and Society*, 33 (2000), pp. 256–86.

Raftopoulos, Brian, 'The crisis in Zimbabwe, 1998–2008', in B. Raftopoulos and A. Mlambo (eds), *Becoming Zimbabwe: A history from the pre-colonial period to 2008* (Harare and Johannesburg, Weaver/Jacana, 2009).

Raftopolous, Brian, 'The threat of "normalising" authoritarianism in Zimbabwe', SPT Brief, Johannesburg, Solidarity Peace Trust, 18 October 2013.

Raftopolous, Brian, 'The 2013 elections in Zimbabwe: The end of an era', *Journal of Southern African Studies,* 39 (2013), pp. 971–88. https://doi.org/10.1080/03057070.2013.862101

Raftopolous, Brian, 'The persistent crisis of the Zimbabwean state', SPT Brief, Johannesburg, Solidarity Peace Trust, 6 September 2016.

Raftopoulos, Brian, *Caught between the Croc and Gucci City* (Cape Town, S.P. Trust, 2017).

Ranger, Terence, 'Nationalist historiography, patriotic history and the history of the nation: The struggle over the past in Zimbabwe', *Journal of Southern African Studies,* 30, 2 (2004), pp. 215–34.

Research & Advocacy Unit, *Zimbabwe since the Elections in July 2013* (Harare, 2017).

Roque, Paula Cristina, *Reform or Unravel?: Prospects for Angola's transition* (Pretoria, ISS, 2017).

Sachikonye, Lloyd, *Zimbabwe's Lost Decade: Politics, development and society* (Harare, Weaver Press, 2012).

Salih, M.A. Mohamed, 'African liberation movement governments and democracy', *Democratization,* 14, 4 (2007), pp. 669–85.

Saunders, Chris, 'Mediation mandates for Namibia's independence (1977–78, 1988)', *African Security*, 10, 3–4 (2017).

Simpson, James G.R., 'Boipatong: The politics of a massacre and the South African transition', *Journal of Southern African Studies,* 38, 3 (2012), p. 623.

Solidarity Peace Trust, *Zimbabwe: The 2018 elections and their aftermath* (Cape Town, 2018).

Solidarity Peace Trust, *Resurgent Authoritarianism: The politics of the January 2019 violence in Zimbabwe* (Cape Town, 2019).

Southall, Roger, 'Introduction: Analysing national liberation movements as governments', in R. Southall (ed.), *Liberation Movements in Power* (Woodbridge, Boydell and Brewer, 2013).

Southall, Roger, 'Bob's Out, the Croc Is In: Continuity or Change in Zimbabwe?', *Africa Spectrum* 17 (2017): 81–94.

Southall, Roger, 'From liberation movement to party machine? The ANC in South Africa', *Journal of Contemporary African Studies*, 32, 3 (2014), pp. 331–48.

Southall, Roger, 'The coming crisis of Zuma's ANC: The party state confronts fiscal crisis', *Review of African Political Economy*, 43, 147 (2016), pp. 73–88.

Southern African Development Community (SADC), *SADC Regional Vulnerability Assessment and Analysis Synthesis Report 2016* (Gaborone, 2016).

Southern African Liaison Office, *South Africa's Relations with Zimbabwe: Pre-colonial to 2006* (Cape Town, 2013).

Sparks, Allister, *Tomorrow is Another Country: The inside story of South Africa's negotiated settlement* (Cape Town and Johannesburg, Jonathan Ball Publishers, 1995).

Stedman, Stephen John, *Peacemaking in Civil War: International mediation in Zimbabwe, 1974–1980* (Boulder, Lynne Rienner, 1991).

Tibane, Elias and Lentsoane, Nomfundo (eds), *South Africa Yearbook 2015/16* (Pretoria, Government Communications, Republic of South Africa, 2016).

Tieku, Thomas Kwasi, Obi, Cyril and Scorgie-Porter, Lindsay, 'The African Peace and Security Architecture: Introduction to the special issue', *African Conflict and Peacebuilding Review*, 4, 2 (2014), pp. 1–10.

Tjønneland, Elling N., 'Making sense of the Southern African Development Community', *African Security Review*, 22, 3 (2013), pp. 190–96.

Truth and Reconciliation Commission, *Truth and Reconciliation Commission Report of South Africa Report* (Cape Town, 1998).

Turner, Thomas, *The Congo Wars: Conflict, myth, and reality* (London, Zed Books, 2007).

Turner, Thomas, 'Will Rwanda end its meddling in Congo?', *Current History*, 112, 754 (2013), p. 188.

Van Nieuwkerk, Anthoni, 'Exploring SADC's evolving peace and security policy framework', in A. Van Nieuwkerk and K. Hofmann (eds), *Southern African Security Review 2013* (Maputo, Friedrich Ebert Stiftung, 2013), pp. 37–53.

Van Nieuwkerk, Anthoni, 'SIPO II: Too little, too late?', *Strategic Review for Southern Africa*, 35 (9 June 2013), pp. 146–53.

Van Nieuwkerk, Anthoni, 'The strategic culture of foreign and security policymaking: Examining the Southern African Development Community', *African Security*, 7, 1 (2014), pp. 45–69.

Van Nieuwkerk, Anthoni and Notshulwana, Mxolisi, 'A critical examination of the key factors and trends shaping Southern African peace and security', in A. van Nieuwkerk and C. Moat (eds), *Southern African Security Review 2015* (Maputo, Friedrich Ebert Stiftung, 2015), pp. 25–44.

Vandome, Christopher, Vines, Alex and Weimer, Markus, *Swaziland: Southern Africa's forgotten crisis* (London, Chatham House, 2013).

Verweijen, Judith, *Stable Instability: Political settlements and armed groups in the Congo* (London, Rift Valley Institute, 2016).

Viegas, Sílvia Leiria, 'Urbanisation and peri-urbanisation in Luanda: A geopolitical and socio-spatial perspective from the late colonial period to the present', *Journal of Southern African Studies*, 42, 4 (2016), pp. 595–618.

Vines, Alex, 'Renamo's rise and decline: The politics of reintegration in Mozambique', *International Peacekeeping*, 20, 3 (2013), pp. 375–93.

Vines, Alex and Weimer, Markus, *Angola: Assessing risks to stability* (Washington, DC, CSIS, 2011).

Vines, Alex, Thompson, Henry, Jensen, Soren Kirk and Azevedo-Harman, Elisabete, *Mozambique to 2018: Managers, mediators and magnates* (London, Chatham House, 2015).

Vlassenroot, Koen and Mathys, Gillian, '"It's not all about the land": Land disputes and conflict in the eastern Congo', Rift Valley Institute, PSRP Briefing Paper 14 (2016).

Weimer, Markus, *The Peace Dividend: Analysis of a decade of Angolan indicators, 2002–12* (London, Chatham House, 2012).

Weiss, Herbert and Carayannis, Tatiana, 'Reconstructing the Congo', *Journal of International Affairs*, 58, 1 (2004), pp. 115–23.

Wiegink, Nikkie, '"It will be our time to eat": Former Renamo combatants and big-man dynamics in central Mozambique', *Journal of Southern African Studies*, 41, 4 (2015).

Williams, Paul D., 'Reflections on the evolving African Peace and Security Architecture', *African Security*, 7, 3 (2014), pp. 147–62.

Witt, Antonia, 'Mandate impossible: Mediation and the return to constitutional order in Madagascar (2009–13)', *African Security*, 10, 3–4 (2017), pp. 205–22.

Wolters, Stephanie, 'Without elections, the DRC's economy will continue to slide', Institute for Security Studies, Pretoria (2017).

Zimbabwe Election Support Network, *Report on the 31 July 2013 Harmonised Elections* (Harare, 2013).

Zimbabwe Election Support Network, *Report on the 30th July 2018 Harmonised Elections* (Harare, 2018).

Zondi, Siphamandla, 'Comprehensive and holistic human security for a post-colonial Southern Africa: A conceptual framework', *Strategic Review for Southern Africa*, 39, 1 (2017), pp. 185–210.

Interviews

Dabengwa, Dumiso, Zimbabwe African People's Union, President, Bulawayo, 30.6.13.

Gwede, Vivid, ZimRights, Communications and Publicity Officer, interviewed by Gideon Chitanga, Harare, 20.5.17.

Kanyenze, Godfrey, Labour & Economic Development Institute, Harare, 09.8.13.

Macamo, Elísio, University of Basel, Basel, 22.11.17.

Makoni, Simba, President of Mavambo/Kusile/Dawn, Former SADC Executive Secretary, Harare, 15.3.13.

Mandaza, Ibbo, Southern African Political Economy Studies Trust, Political Scientists, Harare, 6.11.13.

Masarira, Linda, Zimbabwe Women in Politics Alliance, Director, interviewed by Gideon Chitanga, Harare, 18.5.17.

Masingi, Lucy, Youth Empowerment & Transformation Trust, Director, 16.6.17.

Matondi, Prosper, Director of Ruzivo Trust, Harare, 19.7.13.

Mazarire, Gerald Chikozo, Midlands University, Lecturer, 25.10.13.

Mkwananzi, Promise, #Tajamuka, Leader, interviewed by Gideon Chitanga, Harare, 19.5.17.

Mswelanto, Thilani, Crisis in Zimbabwe Coalition, Director, interviewed by Gideon Chitanga, Harare, 23.5.17.

Mufamadi, Sydney, Republic of South Africa, Head of Mbeki Facilitation Team, Minister of Local Government, Soweto, 14.3.14.

Nathan, Laurie, Professor at University of Notre Dame, interview via email, 2.12.17.

Ndlela, Daniel, Economist with Zimconsult and Adviser to the Minister of Finance, Harare, 30.10.13.

Ndlovu-Gatsheni, Sabelo, University of South Africa, interview via Skype, 2.12.17.

Nyakudya, Munyaradzi, University of Zimbabwe, interview via email, 1.12.17.

Péclard, Didier, University of Geneva, interview via email, 8.12.17.

Udelsmann-Rodrigues, Cristina, Nordic Africa Institute, Uppsala University, interview via email, 11.12.17.

Van Nieuwkerk, Anthoni, University of the Witwatersrand, interview via email, 12.12.17.

Wadzanai, Mangoma, Vendors Initiative for Social & Economic Transformation, Director, interviewed by Gideon Chitanga, Harare, 23.5.17.

Witt, Antonia, Hessische Stiftung Friedens & Konfliktforschung, Post-doc, via skype, 12.12.17.

Zambara, Webster, Institute for Justice and Reconciliation, interview via email, 10.12.17.

Primary Sources

ANCWL, ANC Statement on the DA Motion to Dissolve Parliament, 10.8.17.

AU, African Charter on Democracy, Elections and Governance, 2007, Art. 2–3.

AU, Constitutive Act of the African Union, 2002, Art. 3–4.

Global Political Agreement, Agreement between the Zimbabwe African National Union-Patriotic Front (ZANU-PF) and the two Movement for Democratic Change (MDC) Formations, on Resolving the Challenges Facing Zimbabwe, 15.9.08, Harare, http://archive.kubatana.net/docs/demgg/mdc_zpf_agreement_080915.pdf, 3.1.14.

Indigenisation and Economic Empowerment (General) Regulations, Gazetted 29.1.10, First Schedule, Form IDG 01.

SADC Election Observer Mission, 'Preliminary Statement', Harare, 2.8.13, 17.

SADC Organ Troika Communiqué, Luanda, 21.11.17.

SADC, 30th Jubilee Ordinary Summit Communiqué, Windhoek, 20.8.10, Para 32.

SADC, 32nd Summit Communiqué, Maputo, 18.8.12, Para 24.

SADC, 33rd Summit Communiqué, Lilongwe, 18.7.13.

SADC, 34th Summit Communiqué, Victoria Falls, 18.8.14

SADC, 35th Summit Communiqué, Gaborone, 18.8.17.

SADC, 36th Summit Communiqué, Mbabane, 31.8.16.

SADC, Double Troika Communiqué, Maputo, 14.1.10.

SADC, Double Troika Summit Communiqué, Pretoria, 15.9.17.

SADC, Executive Secretary Stergomena Lawrence Tax, SADC Congratulates His Excellency Emmerson Dambudzo Mnangagwa, President of the Republic of Zimbabwe, Gaborone, 24.11.17.

SADC, Extraordinary Summit Communiqué, Windhoek, 20.5.11. Paras 7–8.

SADC, Principles and Guidelines Governing Democratic Elections, 2004.

SADC, Protocol on Politics, Defence and Security Cooperation, Blantyre, 14.8.01, Art. 1.

SADC, Revised Edition of the Strategic Indicative Plan for the Organ, Maputo, 2010, 23–53.

SADC, SADC Organ Troika plus Council Chairperson Ministerial Meeting discusses the Political Situation in Zimbabwe, Press Release, 16.11.17.

SADC, SADC Selected Economic and Social Indicators 2016, Gaborone, 2017, http://www.sadc.int/information-services/sadc-statistics

SADC, *SADC Statistical Yearbook 2014*, http://www.sadc.int/information-services/sadc-statistics

SADC, SADC Statistical Yearbook 2015, http://www.sadc.int/information-services/sadc-statistics

SADC, Strategic Indicative Plan for the Organ for Politics, Defence and Security Cooperation, Gaborone, 2002.

SADC, Summit Communiqué, Pretoria, 20.8.17.

SADC, Treaty of the Southern African Development Community, 2001.

The Economist, Democracy Index 2016, https://infographics.economist.com/2017/DemocracyIndex/, 1.12.17

Veritas, The Protocol on the SADC Tribunal, Bill Watch 24/2014, Harare, 10.11.14.

News publications

AP NEWS, 'Zimbabwe inquiry finds army, police killed 6 during protest', 18.12.18.

Business Day, 'ANC will rule SA until Jesus comes back, says Zuma', 15.3.04.

Business Day, 'Mugabe unveils five-year plan to save Zimbabwe economy', 23.10.13.

Business Day, 'Africa's richest woman gets fired', 15.11.17.

Business Day, 'Angola's Sonangol investigates misconduct by Isabel Dos Santos', 20.12.17.

EWN Eyewitness News, 'Zuma holds off on Zim visit after meeting Mnangagwa', 22.11.17.

Chronicle, 'Govt relaxes regulations on second hand clothes imports', 19.1.17.

Chronicle, 'Mujuru forms new party', 4.3.17.

The Economist, 'Why the ANC will win South Africa's election, despite governing poorly', 7.5.14.

The Economist, 'South Africa has one of the world's worst education systems', 7.1.17.

Financial Gazette, 'Crisis in crisis coalition', 11.12.14.

Financial Gazette, 'Joice Mujuru's party splits', 9.2.17.

Financial Mail, 'When fear loses power', 14.7.16.

Financial Times, 'Angola's new president defies critics to shake up dos Santos elite', 8.11.17.

Financial Times, 'South Africa envoys meet Mugabe in bid to end Zimbabwe's crisis', 16.11.17.

The Guardian, 'Togo footballers were attacked by mistake, Angolan rebels say', 11.1.10.

The Guardian, 'Joice Mujuru: The woman threatening to topple Robert Mugabe's ruling party', 28.7.15.

The Guardian, 'Mozambique fell prey to the promise of fabulous wealth – now it can't pay nurses', 27.1.17.

The Guardian, 'Morgan Tsvangirai, Zimbabwe opposition leader, dies aged 65', 14.2.18.

Herald, 'ZANU-PF DCC elections postponed', 10.1.12.

Herald, 'Where are the NGOs?', 17.10.13.

Herald, 'Time for patriotic think-tanks', 6.11.13.

Herald, 'Manipulation – Bane of the west', 17.12.13.

Herald, 'ZANU-PF expels Joice Mujuru', 3.4.15.

Herald, 'Cyber Crime Bill: The details', 17.8.16.

Herald, 'President resigns!', 22.11.17.

Herald, 'The operation to restore legacy', 5.12.17.

IOL, 'Pastor spreads word of Zimbabwe's plight', 3.8.16.

Holland, Heidi, 'ANC grows older but not wiser', *The Star*, 3.1.12.

Jeune Afrique, 'Angola: plusieurs morts dans des affrontements entre l'armée et les rebelles du Cabinda', 15.2.17.

Mail & Guardian, 'Zim general's death', 29.3.12.

Mail & Guardian, 'Oil-rich Cabinda the poorer for it', 28.9.12.

Mail & Guardian, 'Zimbabwe's embattled NGO sector feels pinch', 30.5.14.

Mail & Guardian, 'Grand coalition imminent in Zimbabwe', 17.4.14.

Mail & Guardian, 'Morgan Tsvangirai "suspended" by MDC', 27.4.14.

Mail & Guardian, 'Endgame looms for Tsvangirai', 2.5.14.

Mail & Guardian, 'Tsvangirai beats Biti in grassroots support', 09.5.14.

Mail & Guardian, 'Fast forward to a new Zimbabwe', 11.7.14.

Mail & Guardian, 'Kidnapping rattles Zim activists', 13.3.15.

Mail & Guardian, 'Angolan rebels claim to have killed 30 troops; expecting "massive military invasion" from government', 24.3.16.

Mail & Guardian, 'Turbulent Zim faces a grim 2017', 15.12.16.

The New Age, 'Zimbabwe lifts ban on imports', 21.5.17.

New York Times, 'Robert Mugabe, in speech to Zimbabwe, refused to say if he will resign', 11.11.17.

NewsDay, 'MDC-T suspends Elton Mangoma', 19.2.14.

NewsDay, 'Mangoma takes MDC-T to court', 23.3.14.

NewsDay, 'Police search for kidnapped journalist', 11.3.15.

NewsDay, 'Local EU statement on the abduction of Itai Dzamara', 9.6.15.

NewsDay, 'ZimAsset, a failed economic policy', 20.9.17.

NewsDay, 'Mujuru, Biti, Dabengwa form own coalition', 23.9.17.

NewsDay, 'Mugabe in shock cabinet reshuffle', 10.10.17.

NewsDay, 'MDC Alliance root for Chamisa', 15.1.18.

NewsDay, 'MDC Alliance leaders in crisis meeting', 6.2.18.

News24, 'DA a Trojan Horse of apartheid, says ANC', 26.7.16.

Reuters, 'Rebels alive and kicking in Angolan petro-province, oil workers say', 14.6.17.

Reuters, 'Zimbabwe opposition reunites to challenge Mugabe', 05.08.17.

Reuters, 'Zimbabwe's Mugabe names "The Crocodile" Mnangagwa as deputy', 10.12.14.

The Standard, 'Is Itai Dzamara the dreamer we lack?', 18.11.14.

The Standard, 'Does Dzamara's approach work in Zim?', 23.11.14.

The Standard, 'Police crush Occupy Africa Unity protest', 12.6.16.

The Standard, 'ZimAsset targets elusive', 17.7.16.

The Star, 'The unassuming hero of a revolution', 9.7.16.

The Star, 'Zimbabweans in anti-bond notes riot', 4.8.16.

The Star, 'Zim army warns cyber protesters: Head declares war on activists using social media "as weapon"', 6.8.16.

The Star, '#ThisFlag pastor arrested at Zim airport but still vlogging', 3.2.17.

Sunday Times, 'We are fed up and we are not afraid', 10.7.16.

Zimbabwe Independent, 'NGOs, MDC-T hard hit by funding cut', 18.10.13.

Zimbabwe Independent, 'Diamond firms in comeback talks', 15.12.17.

The Zimbabwean, 'Suspected security operatives scare YAT', 25.7.13.

The Zimbabwean, 'CIDA leaving Zim, 29.10.13.

The Zimbabwean, 'I won't be pushed says Lewanika', 28.1.15.

Ziminsky, Paul, 'Marange may not be the world's largest diamond producer for much longer', *London Mining Journal*, May 2014.

Databases

International Crisis Group (ICG), Crisis Watch Database: Angola, 30.9.17, www.crisisgroup.org/crisiswatch/database

World Bank, Angola poverty headcount ratio at $1.9 a day (2011 PPP) (% of population), https://data.worldbank.org/indicator/SI.POV.DDAY?locations=AO

World Bank, World Data Bank: World Development Indicators, 2016.

Index

About the Policy Dialogue Series

The Nordic Africa Institute Policy Dialogue Series is intended for strategists, analysts and decision-makers in foreign policy, aid and development. It aims to inform decision-making and the public debate.

The Policy Dialogue publications are generally written by researchers and based on their original research, but can also include contributions from experts and analysts with a perspective from outside the academic world. The opinions expressed are those of the authors and do not necessarily reflect the views of the Institute.

The series aims to offer a deepened understanding of a current topic, with an explicit purpose of giving policy relevant advice.

A list of previous titles in the Policy Dialogue Series can be found below:

1. Havnevik, K., Bryceson, D., Birgegård, L.-E., Matondi, P., & Beyene, A. (2007). African Agriculture and The World Bank : Development or Impoverishment?

2. Zack-Williams, A., & Cheru, F. (2008). The quest for sustainable development and peace : the 2007 Sierra Leone elections.

3. Utas, M., Persson, M., & Coulter, C. (2008). Young female fighters in African wars : conflict and its consequences.

4. Utas, M. (2009). Sexual abuse survivors and the complex of traditional healing : (G) local prospects in the aftermath of an African war.

5. Eriksson Baaz, M., & Stern, M. (2011). La complexité de la violence : Analyse critique des violences sexuelles en République Démocratique du Congo (RDC).

6. Vogiazides, L. (2012). 'Legal Empowerment of the Poor' versus 'Right to the City' : Implications for access to housing in urban Africa.

7. Vainio, A. (2012). Market-based and Rights-based Approaches to the Informal Economy : A comparative analysis of the policy implications.

8. Eriksson Baaz, M., & Utas, M. (Eds.). (2012). Beyond "Gender and Stir" : Reflections on gender and SSR in the aftermath of African conflicts.

9. Gelot, L., & de Coning, C. (Eds.). (2012). Supporting African peace operations.

10. Nlandu Mayamba Mbuya, T. (2013). Building a Police Force 'for the good' in DR Congo : Questions that still haunt reformers and reform beneficiaries.

11. Follér, M.-L., Haug, C., Knutsson, B., & Thörn, H. (2013). Who is responsible? : Donor-civil society partnerships and the case of hiv/aids work.

12. Adetula, V. A. O., Bereketeab, R., & Jaiyebo, O. (2016). Regional economic communities and peacebuilding in Africa : the experiences of ECOWAS and IGAD.

13. Bereketeab, R. (2019). The Ethiopia-Eritrea Rapprochment : Peace and Stability in the Horn of Africa.

All titles can be downloaded in full text for open access. Please visit NAI's online research publication database DiVA at http://nai.diva-portal.org.

www.ingramcontent.com/pod-product-compliance
Ingram Content Group UK Ltd.
Pitfield, Milton Keynes, MK11 3LW, UK
UKHW061028310726
14090UKWH00027B/360

* 9 7 8 9 1 7 1 0 6 8 5 3 8 *